CAMBRIDGE LIBRARY COLLECTION

Books of enduring scholarly value

Printing and Publishing History

The interface between authors and their readers is a fascinating subject in its own right, revealing a great deal about social attitudes, technological progress, aesthetic values, fashionable interests, political positions, economic constraints, and individual personalities. This part of the Cambridge Library Collection reissues classic studies in the area of printing and publishing history that shed light on developments in typography and book design, printing and binding, the rise and fall of publishing houses and periodicals, and the roles of authors and illustrators. It documents the ebb and flow of the book trade supplying a wide range of customers with products from almanacs to novels, bibles to erotica, and poetry to statistics.

The Methods of Publishing

Samuel Squire Sprigge (1860–1937) was a qualified physician who worked for The Lancet from 1892 and was editor from 1909 until his death. He published several books including a history of the journal and its founder, and a volume of essays, Physic and Fiction. The Methods of Publishing first appeared in 1890 and is Sprigge's passionate contribution to the late nineteenth-century discussion on how the question of literary property is best resolved. Sprigge argues that this matter is often treated in a cavalier manner that disadvantages authors, particularly in the relationship between publisher and author. In his view, book prices are too low, copyright protection for authors is insufficient, the royalty system is in chaos, and authors do not obtain a fair share of profits. He proposes that literary property questions be treated with the same legal formality and protection as is found in other business dealings.

T0371269

The Methods of Publishing

SAMUEL SQUIRE SPRIGGE

CAMBRIDGE UNIVERSITY PRESS

Cambridge, New York, Melbourne, Madrid, Cape Town, Singapore,
São Paolo, Delhi, Dubai, Tokyo

Published in the United States of America by Cambridge University Press, New York

www.cambridge.org
Information on this title: www.cambridge.org/9781108009188

© in this compilation Cambridge University Press 2009

This edition first published 1890
This digitally printed version 2009

ISBN 978-1-108-00918-8 Paperback

THE METHODS OF PUBLISHING.

"We demand for Literary Property the same jealousy and the same resolution to obtain just treatment as prevails in all other branches of business."—*Report of the Society for* 1889.

BY

S. SQUIRE SPRIGGE,

M.B. CANTAB.

LONDON:

Published for the Incorporated Society of Authors,

BY

HENRY GLAISHER, 85 STRAND W.C

1890.

CONTENTS.

———◆———

THE SOCIETY OF AUTHORS (Incorporated).

PRESIDENT.

THE RIGHT HON. THE LORD TENNYSON, D.C.L.

COUNCIL.

SIR EDWIN ARNOLD, K.C.S.I.
ALFRED AUSTIN.
ROBERT BATEMAN.
SIR HENRY BERGNE, K.C.M.G.
WALTER BESANT.
AUGUSTINE BIRRELL, M.P.
R. D. BLACKMORE.
REV. PROF. BONNEY, F.R.S.
LORD BRABOURNE.
JAMES BRYCE, M.P.
P. W. CLAYDEN.
EDWARD CLODD.
W. MARTIN CONWAY.
MARION CRAWFORD.
OSWALD CRAWFURD, C.M.G.
THE EARL OF DESART.
A. W. DUBOURG.
JOHN ERIC ERICHSEN, F.R.S.
PROF. MICHAEL FOSTER, F.R.S.
HERBERT GARDNER, M.P.
RICHARD GARNETT, LL.D.
EDMUND GOSSE.

H. RIDER HAGGARD.
THOMAS HARDY.
PROF. E. RAY LANKESTER, F.R.S.
J. M. LELY.
REV. W. J. LOFTIE, F.S.A.
F. MAX-MÜLLER, LL.D.
GEORGE MEREDITH.
HERMAN C. MERIVALE.
J. C. PARKINSON.
THE EARL OF PEMBROKE AND MONT-
    GOMERY.
SIR FREDERICK POLLOCK, BART., LL.D.
WALTER HERRIES POLLOCK.
A. G. ROSS.
GEORGE AUGUSTUS SALA.
W. BAPTISTE SCOONES.
G. R. SIMS.
J. J. STEVENSON.
JAS. SULLY.
WILLIAM MOY THOMAS.
H. D. TRAILL, D.C.L.
EDMUND YATES.

Hon. Counsel—E. M. UNDERDOWN, Q.C.

Auditor—REV. C. H. MIDDLETON-WAKE, F.L.S.

COMMITTEE OF MANAGEMENT.

Chairman—WALTER BESANT.

ROBERT BATEMAN.
W. MARTIN CONWAY.

EDMUND GOSSE.
H. RIDER HAGGARD.
A. G. ROSS.

J. M. LELY.
SIR FREDERICK POLLOCK.

Solicitors.

MESSRS. FIELD, ROSCOE & CO., Lincoln's Inn Fields.

Secretary—S. SQUIRE SPRIGGE.

OFFICES.

4, PORTUGAL STREET, LINCOLN'S INN FIELDS, W.C.

PREFACE.

THE aim of this book is to arouse a general feeling that there is sound good sense in the demand made in the Report of the Society of Authors for 1889.

"*We demand*," the Report ran, "*for Literary Property the same jealousy and the same resolution to obtain just treatment as prevails in all other branches of business.*"

By this statement I hope to escape the imputation of having failed to do anything which I have never tried to do.

There are in the office of the Society of Authors records of publishing undertaken upon every conceivable and inconceivable plan. All, however, fall under one of these five heads :—(1) SALE OUT-RIGHT, (2) LIMITED SALE, (3) THE HALF-PROFIT SYSTEM, (4) THE ROYALTY SYSTEM (with certain variations), and (5) PUBLICATION BY COMMISSION (also with certain variations).

And under these five heads, the enquiry into the methods of publishing is conducted.

It would seem that the peculiar, unbusiness-like, and but too frequently disgraceful manner with which Literary Property is treated has its origin in the two facts—(1), that the existence of this property is not generally realised ;[*]

---

[*] Its existence has been denied *in toto* on the ground that all ideas are free, so that no one can claim a monopoly in them. The assertion appears to have been made in all gravity.

and (2), that, where realised, its value can only with
difficulty be estimated.

As a consequence the law regulating a property, which
appears even to its possessors so vague and ill-defined, is
in its turn obscure, incomplete, and inconclusive.

One preliminary chapter has, therefore, been devoted
to a brief consideration of the nature of Literary Property,
and another to a brief demonstration of the fact that an
approximate estimate of its value in particular cases can
often be arrived at.

Of all the charges in a publisher's account, the two
which authors find it hardest to believe in are those for
advertisement, and those for "author's corrections." In
each case the author's resentment naturally follows his
inability to understand the account. He sees but one thing,
that he is required to implicitly trust his publisher, as no
vouchers or details are forthcoming. All may go well. On
the contrary, something may happen which rightly or
wrongly shakes the profound confidence which is thus
demanded of the author, and straightway he believes that
he is being cheated. Again, certain ways of dealing with
"Remainder-stock" have led frequently to much annoy-
ance.

A large proportion of the smaller complaints received
at this office have arisen out of some irregularity under one
or other of these three heads. A separate chapter has,
therefore, been devoted to the discussion of each.

There is no intention here to make an attack upon
publishers as a class, or upon any individual publisher. This
is a protest against the methods by which the disposal
of an enormously valuable property is effected.

These methods, however, will exist until the contracts
between author and publisher are prepared with the
business-like care and accuracy which are displayed
in the contracts for the disposal of property in all its
other forms. This desirable result will certainly never be
attained, except in response to the combined resolution of
writers as a body. It is equally certain that it must follow
upon such combined resolution. From the moment that

dealings in Literary Property receive due legal formality and legal protection in their treatment, much of the petty chicanery, so contemptible and yet so vexatious, that is now rife, will come to an end, while the avocation of the serious and extensive rogue will be gone.

At present it is sufficient to find fault with the methods in vogue, for reasons which it is hoped will appear satisfactory.

It will later be the duty of the Society of Authors to submit a scheme for publishing, based upon what may seem after careful consideration of the whole question fair and equitable principles.

Office of the Incorporated Society of Authors,
        4, Portugal Street, W.C.

July, 1890.

CHAPTER I.

LITERARY PROPERTY.

PUBLISHING is the process by which an author brings his work before the public, for whom it has been written, and from whom he expects to reap a return in money, fame, or both.

A man's literary work is, though the fact is too often forgotten, his personal property, which he may use absolutely as he chooses,* over which he alone has control, to sell, to lease, to lend, or to give away. Among the various methods of publishing, there may be included any process. that can be devised for treating such property with a view to obtaining by publicity, a return in money, or in repute, for the labour expended. In fact the schoolboy who stated that "Esau wrote some fables and sold the copyright for a bottle of potash," although hazy as to facts, was merely quoting an agreement, which, by comparison with the actual remuneration frequently received by a modern author, shows that Æsop made by no means a bad bargain.

There are customary methods for dealing with houses or with land, and there are customary methods for dealing with Literary Property. Here the similarity in method ends. Houses and land are placed by their owner at the public disposal according to methods approved by law, and founded upon long custom and experience ; moreover, such disposal is usually, almost invariably,

---

* "Your petitioner may burn or publish his manuscript at his own option, and enjoy a right in and control over his own productions which no press, now or hereafter, can justly press out of him."— Tom Hood, "A Petition to Parliament."

undertaken with legal formality if not under legal advice. Literary Property is dealt with by methods approved neither by equity nor by good sense, founded neither upon custom, nor experience, and protested against from time immemorial by authors. Moreover, these methods have hitherto often been accepted without that legal advice which has been found necessary in all other matters of business. Nay, so far have the customary formalities observed in other affairs been neglected by the author, that even a written agreement has been very often dispensed with.

How is this marked difference of treatment to be accounted for ?

The explanation is as follows :—

Firstly, while Literary Property has as real an existence as any other property, and an author's rights over his work are as undeniable as those over his watch, certain old prejudices or sentimentalisms regarding the author's position towards his public have obscured the rights and damaged the property.

Secondly, the difficulty of estimating the value of particular pieces of Literary Property has given rise to an idea that business methods are out of place in dealing with a property so vague.

Firstly, then, it was at one time considered beneath the dignity of the man of letters to write for money. It was said, and perhaps thought, that genius could never sully its fingers with money, or bargain for remuneration. Genius certainly no longer cherishes this idea. Even in the very days when it prevailed, all the best authors were actually writing for pecuniary reward. Still the assumption that genius and business could not be associated formerly passed unchallenged, and from this sentimentalism has sprung, in part, the fact that the methods of publication now in vogue are calculated to preclude their association for ever.

Again, it has been urged that Literature is, or should be, wholly occupied with the advancement of mankind. The producer, therefore, it has been said, should be only eager to give to the world, that by which the world would be benefited. If it be for the public good that a book should be placed within reach of the public grasp, what right has the producer to dictate terms, to the enrichment of his private purse? This fanciful view of the author's position towards his public has been stated in print,* and though no author could possibly endorse it in its entirety as sensible, many have undoubtedly been actuated by some such sentiment, when agreeing to terms whose iniquity would have been patent to them, if any other form of property had been in question.†

Concerning the proposition, (for this is what it amounts to,) that legislation securing to the author rights in the work of his brain is illogical and improper, because such a monopoly is to the detriment of the public! There is nothing illogical in the author's wish to benefit by his work, however lofty the aim of that work may be. The deviser of anything for the public good has always been held to deserve reward from his fellow citizens—this civilised states have very generally recognised—therefore, the author of a book whose publication is for the public good, and who yet wishes to reap money by it as well as fame, is reasonable in his desire.

---

* "Letters on Copyright."—Henry C. Carey.

† One instance has been offered as a precedent for this view : it is the rule of the Royal College of Physicians against secret remedies. No man can remain a member of the Royal College of Physicians who sells a remedy whose formula is known only to himself. If his science has placed at his disposal knowledge that would enable his fellow physicians to cope more ably with disease, and so to be of more general use to the public, he is bound to make that knowledge the common property of the College, though by so doing he may be surrendering a princely fortune.

But in the doctor's case, scientific men, experts of the same profession, become possessors of certain knowledge, and are thereby enriched as a body both in purse and in repute ; moreover, it was the corporate wealth and learning of the College which placed the discoverer in a position to appreciate his discovery, so that the wealth, thence accruing, rightly returns to the College as a body. In the author's case, even if *he* takes no money, the wealth goes to the publisher, who contributes nothing to the author's task.

Again, it is absurd in the present day to speak of the ordinary *littérateur* as living and working only for the good of the world. He works primarily and properly to get his own living and to advance his own interests. Lastly, the sacrifice by the author of his rights does not benefit the public at large, but the publisher. If the author of a work for the advancement of his fellow men should for conscience sake prefer to receive no reward in money, it is clearly unreasonable that his agent should expect to " take somewhat "* of the public.

Certain real differences between Literary Property and all other kinds of personal property must count as the second cause for the different treatment which Literary Property receives. These are (1) the legal restriction with regard to its sale, and (2) the difficulty of estimating its value. The second of these, as has been already stated, is the only important one.

(1.) *The Copyright Regulations.*—These form the legal recognition that an author has rights in the published work of his brain. If it had not occurred to the benefi- cent to give authors as a privilege some temporary rights in their work, it would probably have been universally assumed that what a man produced by his brain was by Common Law his own for ever.

It is not within the scope of this work to discuss the present condition of the Copyright Law ;- its influence upon the treatment of Literary Property will merely be alluded to. The report of the Royal Copyright Commis- sion in 1878 says, " The Law consists partly of the provisions of fourteen Acts of Parliament, which relate in whole or in part to different branches of the subject, and partly of Common Law principles, nowhere stated in any definite or authoritative way, but implied in a considerable number of reported cases scattered over the law reports."

This condition of the Law affects writers as a body, for their property, which requires peculiar and intelligent

---

* 2 Kings, ch. v., 20, *et seq.*

care for its protection, is thus peculiarly open to depreda-
tion.

No particular book, however, is injured in value by
the fact that in forty-two years or more it becomes public
property. The number of books that remain standard
works and in demand after more than forty years of publication is very small indeed, while it is always open to the
possessor of the copyright to place such a large issue on
the market just before the legal term expires as to exhaust
the value of the book for some years yet to come.

But if the author is not particularly injured by
the fact that his book becomes public property after
a certain term of years, he is injured by the fact that
during that term his rights are ill-defined, and difficult to
ascertain.

(2.) *The alleged uncertainty as to the value of Literary
Property.*—In many cases this uncertainty actually exists.
A work may often be thought well of by one, and condemned
by another. A book, again, which experts admire, the
public may, perhaps, refuse to read, while every year sees
the production of one, at least, whose pecuniary success is
as marked as it was unexpected. Some books are essen-
tially ephemeral ; some few mellow with time ; some, but
very few, are for all time. It is not always possible to
guess to which class a new work belongs. A certain value
is ensured to one book by its style, to another by its
matter, and to a third by its author's name. Any work on
certain subjects will sell ; an admirable work on other subjects can never sell. Successful advertising may start a
bad book, incompetent or dishonest publishing has often
restrained a good one. Briefly, it is obvious that the
money value of any particular work may always be
dependent upon a dozen different reasons.

This variety of the causes tending to influence the
value of Literary Property certainly has much to do with
the author's loose and careless way of conducting his
business. So much, it would seem, has to be taken into
consideration, precaution has to be observed in so many
directions, his property's value is dependent on so many
and such different factors, that finally he decides that no

one can estimate its worth. Therefore, he becomes apathetic towards it.

In this spirit he enters into any contract that is submitted to him, careless of its real meaning, careless of its inevitable result. This, by making it eminently possible for any publisher to cheat an author, makes it eminently probable that some publisher will cheat him. Yet surely this very uncertainty of issue, instead of leading the author to idly despise his work, should embolden him to hope that there may be some one of these many influences acting in his ‚case to make his book a valuable one. So far from considering the likelihood of success to be based upon so many off-chances that it is useless to calculate upon them, surely he should remember that the chances of success are as varied as the chances of failure, and should therefore be prepared to take his due share of the profits, if success should come in his way. There is only one way in which this can be done. The author must have a written agreement with the publishers, the clauses of which he himself understands, securing to himself his rights and his legitimate share of the profits which may accrue, and guarding himself against unjust and fraudulent charges, and unfair deductions from the gross returns. This contract must be entered upon with as much gravity and as much forethought as would be necessarily employed in the disposal of other property. Expert advice is as necessary; business formality as essential.

The uncertainty as to the value of Literary Property, while largely accounting for its loose and careless management, is the strongest argument in favour of placing all transactions or dealings in this property on a sound business basis.

The existence of an author's rights in his work is not generally denied. But, on the other hand, it seems that there is difficulty in understanding and believing in them ; nor are they regarded with the sanctity that his rights in other property would be.

The law of the land recognising his rights is chaotic

The results of ancient prejudices still remain to the author's detriment, while the prejudices themselves have long become obsolete.

Lastly, the only important difference between Literary Property and all other property—a difference in no way affecting its reality, but only its saleability—is the alleged uncertainty of its value. This, while considered by author and publisher alike to be an excuse for loose dealing in Literary Property, on the contrary calls especially for formal legal care in its disposition.

CHAPTER II.

THE VALUE OF THE DIFFERENT FORMS OF LITERARY PROPERTY.

MUCH, then, of the apathy displayed by authors towards their work is caused by their ignorance of the value of that work.   Hence this question :—

Is it impossible to predict the value of a book ?

Not quite impossible.   Certainly it is very rare that the value can be estimated with accuracy, even where the work is from the pen of a well-known author.   But there are many considerations which—if they ever were considered —would go far to clear up the total uncertainty as to value, on which so much stress has always been, and still is, laid.   These considerations it is proposed to briefly mention.

Speaking a little roughly, all books will fall under one or other of the eight divisions that follow.   To each division belong certain characteristics affecting the estimate of its value.

1. BOOKS OF THEOLOGY : *Religious Instruction, Commentary and Controversy.*
2. BOOKS OF EDUCATION : *Technical Works, Science, and Philosophy.*
3. FICTION.
4. BOOKS OF TRAVEL.
5. MEMOIRS.
6. HISTORY AND BIOGRAPHY.
7. BELLES LETTRES : *Essays and Criticism.*
8. POETRY.

I. Books of Theology.

These may be divided into sermons, controversial and doctrinal books, historical, biographical, and story-books.

Sermons have, as a rule, no pecuniary value, unless the position of the author is one that ensures a sale. Those of a divine noted for his eloquence, or of a schoolmaster for his influence, will sell, and sell widely: the most eloquent homilies of the unknown, when put forward in the shape of homilies, secure no sale.

Books controversial and doctrinal, are much fewer than of old, because the controversies have for the most part gone into new ground, where the old reasoner cannot follow them. Scholars and divines no longer wrangle much over the interpretation of a passage or the maintenance of a doctrine, being now more concerned with the upholding of the very foundations on which all religion rests. On the other hand, the introduction into fiction of controversy upon any and all subjects may revive in a new form this kind of religious or irreligious discussion.

As to books which treat of religious subjects from the historical, biographical or geographical point of view, their name is legion, and their success is in some cases enormous. One would like to know, for instance, how many copies of Dr. Smith's "Dictionary of the Bible" have been sold. Every year brings out new books on Bible characters and Bible lands, and they are sold by thousands. Here is a great field for an aspiring author, especially for one who is fitted for his task by some knowledge of the East, of Hebrew, Latin, and Greek, and who has command of the "religious language."

As to religious story books, for these there is an endless demand, and of them an equally endless supply. They are chiefly published by the Society for the Promotion of Christian Knowledge, the Religious Tract Society, and two or three firms which have made this kind of book their speciality, and have done on the whole remarkably well with them. The S. P. C. K. makes £6,000 a year

B

profit, and the other Society £18,000 a year on their publishing business !

This kind of book is generally bought right out by the publisher for sums of money ranging from £5 upwards. Amongst the writers women are in the majority. One religious writer who is prudent enough to keep his work in his own hands is reported to make over £2,000 a-year, but of course this is a very unusual and exceptional case. It serves, however, to show that, not only solid works of theology, but religious fiction, may, under favourable circumstances, become a most valuable property, and to illustrate the necessity of retaining possession of such property, and the folly of parting with it for totally inadequate sums.

II. BOOKS OF EDUCATION.

Under this head are included all *Scientific, Professional, Technical,* and *Scholastic* books.

Some professional and technical works naturally have but a very small sale. These are nearly always produced either at the expense of the author—as are, for instance, most medical treatises—or at the expense of some learned Society.

On the other hand, there is an immense market for school books. The spread of national education is also enormously improving this class of property. Not only has the number of learners increased, but the foundation of a system of standards common to all schools necessitates the use of common class books ; therefore, a good class book may, if it proves successful, have a very large, an enormous sale, up to the day when a better book on the same subject takes the field. The Americans have so far recognised this that they say of the author, whose text book has been adopted by a State for use in the schools, that he has "captured the State." There is no better property than a good school book adopted in the best public schools, and therefore widely used in all schools.

Books of religion and books of instruction have this in common. Not only is the demand for them regular, but they are bought by the public, not hired from the libraries.

A text book on any educational subject, however, has generally but a short life, even if a merry one, owing to the constant changes in methods, theories, and treatment. What is now the value of a book on Chemistry published with the old notation? What, at any rate, for examination purposes, would be the value of a treatise on Surgery or Medicine that did not recognise the "germ-theory" and "antiseptic" remedies? On the other hand, a standard work on Theology should last as long as the beliefs of which it treats.

III. FICTION.

It is generally thought that this is surely the class of books which enjoys the largest circulation, and consequently produces the largest return to the author or to his publisher. Judged by average results, however, fiction is, on the whole, a less valuable property than either of the two classes of work considered before.

The writers who have any circulation at all are few, those who have a large circulation very few, while those whose books never attain to a paying sale are countless. Let it be stated that almost invariably the public judgment is right, and that these failures deserve the neglect which they receive. On the other hand, it is in fiction that we meet generally with those astonishing successes in cases where no success could have been anticipated; and it is these that, by giving so great an element of uncertainty to the future of every new book, have confirmed authors, publishers, and public alike in the idea that the future of a book cannot be predicted.

But the value of even a good novel is generally much more evanescent than that of a good production in the preceding classes. When the libraries have subscribed for their copies, and when the cheaper editions have been at the public's disposal for a few months— and especially when one or two more good novels come into the market—the demand ceases. A very good novel by a very popular author will have a certain annual sale for years, but the rush for it dies away in a few months, only, sadly to say, to be revived by the author's death. The temporary character of a novel's value should not be lost sight of. It is a most important indication of the most judicious way to publish them.

Those who do not know the methods of production think because an immense number of novels are published every year that the money made by their sale must be enormous. It is not generally known that quite three-fourths of the novels published are actually produced at the expense of their authors, and result in no profit whatever except to the publishers, who rightly take good care not to lose by such transactions.

This enormous output of fiction, which has no pecuniary value whatever, will here be entirely disregarded, and only saleable fiction considered.

The value of a novel depends upon three things :—

Its author : whether he be a well-known man or a new man, or one who has already been tried and has failed.

Its aptness: that is to say, there is always a fashion in thought, conversation, views on society, art, and religion. The novel which is *apt* falls in with the prevalent fashion, and so suits the shifting needs of the public. These are the books whose success is very generally attributed to their novelty. The public is ready for a new departure. Several people try to meet the demand. The novelist most in touch with his public succeeds the best.

Its merits : novels succeed by their merits in this sense ; if a novelist can write works that interest, amuse, or move the reader, he will succeed, and will succeed on the merits of his work. Sheer literary merit alone is a factor of much less importance than interest ; but only let the novelist be able to do one of these three things *and* invest the deed with literary merit, and he may safely reckon on becoming the owner of a splendid personal property.

The work of the successful author can, within limits, be estimated in value by deduction from his previous results.

That of the beginner cannot. The assumption on the publisher's part that the latter's work is always valueless is illogical, if only because the successful men must have had a beginning.

Let the beginner by means of an agreement put himself in a position to profit by success, however distant success may appear.

IV. BOOKS OF TRAVEL.

These are sure of a good reception if they are records of exploration personally undertaken in lands about which little or nothing is known. For instance, the papers have lately contained numberless allusions to the new big book of travels, with hints as to the enormous price the fortunate author was to receive from the enterprising publisher. But, as with fiction, so with books of travel, the demand is soon over. Such records generally become out of date in a very short time. It is true that the unknown countries are rapidly decreasing, on the other hand, a new kind of exploration has been established, namely, scientific exploration. Mountains are ascended, and woods are searched in the interests of philanthropy or scientific investigation : the natives are examined for anthropological or sectarian purposes : the languages are studied by philologists. So that for a long time to come the traveller will have plenty to write about.

Little travels, journeys up and down the face of England, if well written, are pretty certain to find some measure of success.

Can any idea be formed as to the pecuniary value of these books before they are issued? It is pretty certain that few travellers ever recover their travelling expenses by writing a book of their experiences. The author of one of the most delightful recent books of minor travels received, for his share of the profit, after what appeared to be a very considerable success, about £30. What the publisher made was rather more than double this sum. The two points to be taken into consideration are, the name of the traveller and the general interest felt in the countries visited. As pure literary art will not sell a novel, so pure scientific record, however new and true, will not sell travels, as travels. It may sell them as scientific works. Many most important works of travel, bearing the imprint of some first-class house, have been published at the author's own expense.

V. MEMOIRS.

These are sometimes very valuable in the present, and may be so in the future. Their value in the future depends upon their literary merit, that is to say, upon their permanence in literature as *belles lettres*, or upon any historical or ethnological significance they may possess. In the present, unless the writer occupies a very notable position, they are apt to be only valuable, if they are sufficiently jocose or abundantly scandalous. As for biographies, there have been of late so many examples of success that they may be said to be a lucrative branch of literature to somebody, and an author who possesses something of the dramatic spirit may well be encouraged to turn his attention in this direction. It would be safe to predict a sale of over 100,000 copies of Lord Beaconsfield's memoirs in three months if they were produced now or soon.

VI. HISTORY.

Here it is necessary that the author should have means and leisure, besides scholarship and the historical faculty. Where these are present success is certain. The names of Freeman, Stubbs, Green, Lecky, Leslie Stephen, and Morley do not suggest failure, while Macaulay is believed to have made over £120,000 by his single work. Every new history of our own empire, or of any portion of it, treated freshly and picturesquely, is always sure to command at least attention. Few are so endowed as to be able to produce such work, but whoever can, and does, may find himself in possession of a valuable property. A recent popular history is known to have produced for its writer, under what we believe was a fair agreement, the sum of £4,000.

VII. BELLES LETTRES.

There is here, at any rate, a practical method of finding the true value of the work. There is always a demand for essays, studies, criticisms, and monographs generally; this is proved by the rapid increase in the number of the periodicals which contain them. But let the author not expect a large sale of his essays when collected and published in a book. Periodicals vary greatly in the literary standard that they require ; hence the value of such work may be roughly estimated by the ease or difficulty with which the author gains access to the pages of a magazine, and to what magazine he gains access. At the same time certain quite recent successes should encourage authors in this admirable branch of literature.

VIII. POETRY.

Two or three living poets make large sums of money ; two or three more make very small sums. The poetical work of all the rest put together is worth almost nothing at all pecuniarily. This especially applies to poetry issued in volume form.

There is a small market for occasional verse in magazines, but the rate of pay does not seem to be very high.

A popular and comparatively successful minor poet has lately recorded that, although he had no difficulty in getting access to the pages of various magazines, he only managed to make £63 9s. in the course of the year, and he had to write thirty-eight different poems to do that. Every now and then a collection of such occasional pieces meets with a good reception.

These are the considerations that should help an author

to arrive approximately at an idea of the worth of his work. They are all perfectly obvious to those who know, so obvious that it seems ludicrous to set them down, yet the conclusions which should be drawn from them are curiously neglected. A clever business man will, when dealing with the work of his brain, sell out-right for a sum totally inadequate a book whose sale may be large and steady for years. Another, also a good business man in other respects, has a book whose value is quite ephemeral, which can never reach a sale of many hundreds. This man will agree without question to receive a share of profits *after* the book reaches a limit which it never can possibly reach. He may defend his action on the ground that the future of his book can in no way be predicted. Yet surely that is the very reason why he should prepare himself, by proper precaution in his agreement, to receive a due share of the profits, however unlikely it may seem to him that any profits should ensue.

The position of the author towards the publisher varies, or should vary, with the value of his work. This the Society of Authors has always recognised, and has often pointed out to authors not themselves so ready to recognise it.

It is evident that whereas many books must have a sure and certain circulation of sufficient size to preclude loss upon their production, many others can have no such circulation predicted for them, while on a third class the loss must be as sure and certain as the gain on the first.

In the first instance the position of the publisher is very clear. He is an agent; his services are only required as an agent, and he should benefit directly in proportion to the sales effected. No capital is required to float the undertaking; the circumstances that have been mentioned as constituting a successful book will float it from the first. All that is required is a faithful agent, so satisfied with his fair proportion of profits, that he will from self-interest, as much as from conscientiousness, do his best to promote sales, and so jealous of his reputation that he will insist upon placing his open books before the eyes of his principal.

Neither in the last instance is there any doubt about the course that should be pursued. The author of a first novel, unless the opinion pronounced upon his work by a competent judge be very favourable, has no business to expect a publisher to produce his book for him without a guarantee against certain loss. Still more must the young poet make up his mind that his work, until he is known, has no pecuniary value whatever. In these cases the author, recognising that the sales may not cover the cost of production, but having good reasons to wish that his work should nevertheless be produced, must take all the risks himself. No one expects a publisher to undertake the issue of a work by which he must lose. All that is demanded is that the publisher's loss should not be magnified, or rather should not have a chance of being magnified ; and this can only be provided against by an agreement being carefully drawn up between the contracting parties in which, among other things, there is a clause binding the publisher to account in detail for the expenditure which he states to have been incurred.

Lastly comes the great middle-class—the books which cannot be expected to have a very large sale, may have only a very small one, and yet are neither condemned from the first to actual failure, nor certain to achieve even the slightest success. Concerning the publication of these works it is sufficient to say that whoever runs the risk should reap a due share in the profits.

Though the exact value of an individual book may be impossible to predict, the amount of uncertainty has been greatly exaggerated.

CHAPTER III.

SALE, OUT-RIGHT AND LIMITED.

In this and the following chapters it is proposed to discuss the various methods of publication now in use ; to point out as far as possible what they mean to the author and what to the publisher, so that in consenting to an agreement the author may know what he is giving away, and what he is receiving in exchange.

The first of these methods and the earliest in history, is the Sale Out-right.

I.—*The Sale Out-right.*

This method is the simplest. The author has a piece of property which he offers for sale, and it would appear to be nobody's business but his own, if he makes a bad bargain. Now there are reasons why the author must very generally make a bad bargain, therefore this method of publishing is not to be recommended under any but the most infrequent circumstances.

The following are the reasons :—

(1.) *Often the author cannot afford to wait, but must take any price rather than no price.*

Everybody is aware that theoretically the producer can choose whether he will take the price offered or not. But everybody also is aware that necessity knows no law, and that the buyer recognises no other right in the producer than what the law allows him—namely, the right to keep his property if he will not sell it.

(2.) *The author is generally ignorant of the real nature of the publisher's risk.*

The production of books has always, and possibly with deliberate design, been shrouded in mystery, so that the author has not been surprised at receiving a pitiful sum for his rights, because he has been led to believe that the publisher has had before him a most expensive, delicate, and almost perilous task.

The Society of Authors has been able to give to its members the history of the production of a book, attaching accurate figures to all the details of publication. From these figures it may be learned that the publisher's risk in producing a book is very much smaller than has been usually represented. No author can make a fair bargain for himself by outright sale—he is not in a position to do so—unless he knows approximately how much it will cost the publisher to produce his work. The publisher may always allege that the risks in his trade are so enormous that he cannot in justice to himself offer more than the small sum, at which perhaps the author has taken exception. How can the author insist upon a better offer, if he is ignorant of the publisher's true risks?

When the technical knowledge of the author is equal to the technical knowledge of the publisher a fair bargain can sometimes be made; until now the author has usually been ignorant, and has usually paid for his ignorance. If he remains ignorant, it is now his own fault.

(3.) *The author is generally ignorant of the value of his work.*

Nobody, not the most experienced publisher, knows with certainty what number of copies of a book, even by the most successful of authors, will be taken by the public. Still the uncertainty is not so great as may appear. It must be remembered that a substantial sum of money is rarely indeed offered except to authors of proved position and popularity, and this only by publishers who know beforehand what he has already done, and can form a very good idea of the minimum circulation of his work. Of course their calculations are based, and rightly, on his minimum circulation for their highest bid.

The following is the practical experience of an author who resolved not to remain ignorant either of his publisher's real risks or of the value of his own books. Moreover he was not compelled to take the first pitiful offer that was made to him. In fact in his case none of the reasons usually accounting for bad bargains prevailed. He entered upon his transactions with open eyes.

He published his first four novels at his own expense. He did not publish them "on commission," according to what we shall find is the usual interpretation of that method, but he had them privately printed, moulded, and bound, and paid the bill himself. Then he took them to a publisher and said, "Account to me for each copy you sell at so much—the difference between that sum and what is received for the books will repay you."

Now all these books were successful, one or two greatly so.

By this method their producer found out for himself— and has since profited by the knowledge—the only facts which can guide an author in his acceptance or refusal of a publisher's offer.

He found out how much his books cost to produce.

He found out their average sale.

He found out the average duration of that sale.

With these facts before him he was able to calculate what returns his book would have brought him under the agreement usually proposed—that is upon some royalty or half-profit system—and to compare them with his returns upon the plan he had adopted.

Next he disposed of the copyrights of one or two— making at the outset a very bad bargain, in that he surrendered for £100 all his rights in a novel of which certainly over 50,000 copies have been sold. Later, how- ever, he found out his proper figure.

The result of this author's practical experience was, that he decided that, if he could get a price beyond a certain limit, he would do best to dispose of his books outright, because the amount of trouble thus saved was so great. He got that price, and there is no doubt that he got it as much because he *knew*, and knew for certain that his books were worth it, as because his publishers thought that they were good books.

This author in no way allows, and the Society of Authors in no way allows, that he ever received his just share of profits, for that is to beg a question which has yet to be discussed, viz.: "What share in the profits of a book *is* the author's just one?" All that his case shows is that the method of outright sale is only satisfactory where the author combines practical knowledge of the details of publishing with either tolerably easy circumstances, or an assured position as a writer; and that then it is only satisfactory because it saves trouble.

There are other inducements to sell a book outright besides the escape from all future troubles. For instance, there have been published of late years a great many series of biographical and critical studies. These are generally attractive volumes priced at about half-a-crown. It is in some cases, and indeed in most, a distinction to be one of the writers of these volumes: in other cases it is an opportunity of bringing to light the results of much reading and research. Payment is generally made at the rate of £100 per volume. That these books are paid for on the ordinary calculation of the value of the highest skilled labour possible, it is absurd to suppose, yet the editors do their best to obtain the author most fitted for the task. What such a man may lose by the low rate of payment, he is supposed to gain by the public recognition that such is his proud position. But these books pay the publishers for otherwise they would not continue to be brought out. In fact it wants a very little arithmetic coupled with the knowlege of the cost of publication, to show that if 10,000 copies be sold the publishers may make three times what they have given the author. And if 20,000 copies are sold they may make seven times as much as the author. Mark also that there is in these cases no risk to be taken by the publisher, as a justification of his lion's share. The subject is selected because it is a likely one. The books form a series, so that if one falls below the average merit, it will still probably be bought for uniformity's sake.   Lastly and chiefly, the author, as we have said, is always a well-known man of letters, whose name ensures a considerable circulation for his work. Some sell more than others, but the risk of any one not selling enough to pay expenses is small indeed.   Of course the publisher has to pay the services of an editor in some cases.

As a matter of daily practice the great majority of publishers do not buy books at all ; some because they have not enough capital ; some because they have not the knowledge or the sagacity necessary for purchase, which, in certain hands, is a highly speculative and risky game. They offer their customers terms, the nature of which will be described ; but they do not buy.

Sometimes when a book is about to be published which is quite certain to have a great and immediate success, the author will receive what, in his innocence, he will consider a just, even a generous, offer for it.   One instance of such generosity will suffice.   A short time ago such a book was ready for publication, and a certain firm of publishers offered a certain sum down—a large sum—in four figures. The author was on the point of concluding what seemed to him an offer boundlessly liberal, when, unfortunately for the open-handed publishers, he talked over the matter with another publisher.   He then learnt for the first time the exact meaning of " cost of production," " trade price," and " probable sales."   He returned fortified with this information, and the result was that the generosity of the publishers had to be *multiplied by three* !   This true story illustrates the spirit in which such offers are sometimes made.   Let the author remember a maxim common among business men, " *There is no friendship in business.*"   The more an author recognises this maxim, the more respect and the better treatment he will get from his publisher under the present methods.

We will go down a step.   There are two classes of work, reaching the public by the method under discussion, which are not from the pens of well-known men—children's story-books and penny novelettes.

There are published every year immense numbers of one volume stories, of the kind adapted for children, for schools, and for simple presents and prizes. Several firms make this kind of business their speciality, and do very well with it. Some few are believed to have made very large fortunes indeed by the production and sale of such books.

The following figures, supplied by a writer who worked for many years for such a firm, shows why they thrive. Their way is the way of the sweater, the grasping unscrupulous sweater, careless of any rights that the law does not enforce, with no thought of justice, no touch of pity for the poor workwoman—the author is nearly always a lady —who is compelled by stern necessity to take his offer, whatever it may be. This was a religious firm. The stories in question were all refined and lofty in tone ; they were also readable and mildly exciting. Out of eleven books the author received for one—this a solid historical work—£70 ; for four £50 each ; for one £45 ; for one £35 ; for one £28 ; for three £20 each. There was little or nothing to account for the difference in price : that seemed ruled by caprice. The sweaters got the lady, in fact, as cheaply as they could. One of these volumes, that for which she got £45, has been subjected to a little calculation as to cost, sale, and profit. The figures show that a sale of 10,000 copies means a profit of £155 to the publishers and of £45 to the author. This is a firm for business avowedly Christian! Of course if the sale is 20,000 or more, the iniquity of the transaction becomes tenfold worse.

Again, everybody knows the "Novelettes," the wonderful pennyworth of excitement and horror which form the staple reading of the lower-class British female. They are sold by hundreds of thousands. They cost to produce a small fraction under a halfpenny, they realise to the publisher a small fraction over a halfpenny. This seems little, but the sale is enormous. The publisher gets enviably rich, and it is so thriving a trade that one wonders there

is not more competition.   The sums paid to the authors
of these works vary from £2 10s. to £10 for a novelette
of 30,000 words—say, on an average, £5 a-piece.   That is
twenty-five words a penny, without counting anything for
invention, construction, and grace of style.   There may be
some publishers of "penny-dreadfuls" who pay more—
one hopes there are.   There is certainly one person who
sometimes pays less, for he has been known to lay pre-
datory hands on a MS. and pay nothing at all.   Unwilling-
ness on the part of his victims to take legal proceedings
has so far protected him.

Is the method of " Out-right Sale" a satisfactory one to Authors ?

The well-known author finds it to have some merits, in
that it saves trouble and annuls all chance of litigation, not
because he gets good prices by it.*
The other authors all find it disastrous.
The young writer who sells his book outright for (say)
£20 may consider himself fortunate, because it so rarely
happens that such an offer is made : but if he accepts it
from anybody save a very first-class firm, to appear on
whose lists is a material advantage, he is *foolish*.   Such
an offer means that his book is saleable.   If he really

---

* Publishers have occasionally made bad bargains under this
method.   It is doubtful if the publishers of "Endymion" or "Daniel
Deronda " have ever seen their money back.
In such cases it should be remembered that the money, if lost,
was lost in reasonable speculation, and that such offers would never
be made or expected, if it was not well known that enormous profits
had been derived from previous books by the same authors.   Did the
authors always get their due share of those profits ?
Again—publishers have occasionally, when a novel picked up for
a song has achieved an enormous success, sent the author a cheque.
There is no intention to detract from the merits of so graceful an
act, nevertheless it helps to make clear that a method of publishing is badly wanted, by which the author should obtain the
results of a success because he has earned it, not because the publisher
is generous.

understood that the cost of producing this work would
possibly be under £100, and that the profit derived from
it possibly over £500, he would think twice before com-
pleting such a bargain.   To the youngest writer, in
possession of such facts, it would occur that he ought to
receive a larger share of the profits.

The unfortunate producers of children's story-books and
" Novelettes " must feel that their efforts are inadequately
rewarded.

The following advertisement appeared quite recently in
the " Athenæum."   " To Authors.—*Literary Prizes.*—An
old-established firm of publishers is prepared to offer the
sums of £50, £30 and £20 for three approved MSS. of
tales, historical or otherwise, not to exceed 300 pp. of
ordinary print, of a healthy tone, suitable for boys and
girls ranging from ten to fifteen."

It is the heading to which exception should be taken.
It well illustrates the spirit in which certain firms, even
old-established ones, deal with authors.   In what possible
sense can £20 or £50 be *a prize* to an author who has to
compose and surrender in exchange for it a book of 300
pages, healthy in tone and interesting in matter?   Books
for boys and books for girls may daily be written of the
required length that are not worth £20, but that is beside
the question, which is, " How is £20 or £50 a prize to the
author of a good book?"   Is this old-established firm a
little off its balance, a little exalted, at the idea of paying
any money at all for a book?

II.—*Limited Sale.*

An author under this method may sell his rights :—

(1) For a limited period of time.
(2) For a limited number of copies.

Before agreeing to either method he should take
advice.

(1) *For a Limited Period of Time.*

This is not a usual mode of publishing, but it is the fairest for the author of any yet in vogue. While the publisher in return for the payment he has made to the author, and for his trouble and expense in the production, receives all the proceeds of the first demand for the book, later on the author re-enters into possession of his copyright, and has the satisfaction of feeling that he has not disposed for a small sum down of a property that annually makes him some return.

In selling the right for a limited period it must be remembered that an eminent judge has held that, although the agreement was only for a certain period, if the publisher had stock over, he was authorised to go on selling them. This opinion seems absolutely unjust, but it has never been reversed. Every such agreement, therefore, under this method, must contain a clause meeting this point, either by providing for an absolute cessation of the sale by a certain date, or by granting facilities by which the author can obtain the "remainder stock" at a reasonably low price.

(2) *For a Limited Number of Copies.*

The right to sell a limited number of copies can only be given in return for the right to ascertain that no more than that number of copies have been sold, *i.e.*, the author or his representative must be able to see the printer's bill, and, if necessary, to count the publisher's stock. But the insertion of a clause providing this for the author has been regarded as an insult, and was regarded so, I believe, until the Society of Authors claimed it as a right.

In one case which has come before the Society of Authors, publishing under this method has led to litigation, because no such clause was present in the agreement.

The work was a technical one, and appeared to bear on its face the chance of a large circulation.

The author had reason to believe that his publisher had

sold more copies than he had been authorised to, and went to law.

He then proved that the publisher had printed and issued a certain number of copies over and above the stipulated number.*

Again it was in a transaction of this kind that the following episode occurred. A certain firm, universally believed to be respectable, made the following bargain with a lady. She was to write for them a story of a certain length; she was to receive £15 down for "the first edition," and if there was any demand for a second edition she was to receive £10 more.

She believed that the first edition meant 1,000 copies, and she agreed. (Observe, by the way, the nature of the bargain. Whatever the success of the book she was to give over everything after the first edition for £10! to sell what might prove a perennial stream for £10!) The publisher, however, possibly knowing that this kind of book seldom went beyond 2,000 copies in his hands, made his first edition of that number. The event proved as he expected ; that is to say, if there was any demand for more, it was not enough to justify him, he considered, in bringing out a new edition. Therefore the poor lady got her £15 and no more. The publisher got for his share about £45. This case shows the necessity of clearly specifying exactly what is meant by an edition. If this lady had been provided with a proper agreement, she would at any rate not have had to submit to this disappointment, and might possibly have been £10 richer. Probably she regarded her agreement as the kind of thing that the publishers would look after, and save her the trouble.

---

* "——un fameux Libraire. Il a depuis peu imprimè un Livre qui a eu beaucoup de succès. En le mettant au jour, il promit á l'Auteur de lui donner cinquante pistoles, s'il réimprimoit sont ouvrage, et il rêve actuellement qu'il en fait une seconde édition sans l'en avertir." Le Diable Boiteux, vol. iii., c. 3. From which it appears that the possibility of this occurrence has long been recognised.

Is the method of "Limited Sale" a satisfactory one to writers?

(1.) Where the author sells his rights for a definite time it seems that if any market remained for the book, when it again became the author's property, the publisher could always spoil that market. He can sell any stock he has over. What is to prevent him at present from arranging that that stock should be a large one, by producing a new edition just before the author regains the copyright?

(2.) Where the author sells his rights for a certain number of copies, the objection is still more patent. This method can only be made into a satisfactory business transaction by a clause in the agreement giving the author access to the publisher's books. Such a precaution may, when taken against many houses, be so unnecessary as almost to appear vexatious. But there are publishers whose records call for the precaution, while to make distinction is impossible. Moreover, in all other business transactions, it would follow as a matter of course upon the agreement that either party should be placed in a position to satisfy himself that the agreement has been kept.

CHAPTER IV.

III.—THE HALF-PROFIT SYSTEM.

CONCERNING this system, Douglas Jerrold said that he liked it "because it never led to any division between author and publisher."

This is the usual proposition. The publisher says to the author, "Give me your MS.; I will publish it without any risk to yourself, in a form creditable to my house, worthy of the work, and without delay. I will pay the whole or half the cost of production. I will give it proper advertisement. In return we will share all the profits."

Nothing can at first sight seem simpler. The book trade is uncertain, for though there are sundry indications of the future value of a book, the profits of no book can be accurately estimated before it appears. The publisher, moreover, appears to be running great and unknown risks —the very word risk conjures up an awful spectre before the author's eyes. As a matter of fact a publisher usually only offers to "take the risk," when he is very certain that there is none to take. The author, who is ignorant of this fact, with the recklessness towards literary property which we are always pointing out and reprobating, signs the agreement sent to him almost without reading it, if there be any agreement; or accepts the letter, if the proposal is by letter, or even agrees verbally, without the trouble of asking for so much as a letter. In each case he transfers his property to the publisher with a kind of shame, as if he were trespassing upon a stranger's good nature, not employing an agent to work for him.

Let us examine some of the agreements usually sent to authors on Half-Profits terms.

In the first place it is a usual — though a most

objectionable—term of the half-profit agreement that the author should cede his copyright out and out to the publisher. Where the author is selling his property, and clearly understands what he is going to get for his property, he may, as has been said, often make a bad bargain. But when he is asked to give his copyright in return for benefits still in the uncertain future he is asked to agree to a very foolish and one-sided proceeding. In return the publisher sometimes takes the whole cost of producing the work. But whatever fraction of the cost he does take, it is understood to be in consideration of that cost that the demand for the copyright is made. As soon as any money comes in it is applied in the first instance to repaying the cost of production, so that the author does not receive anything until the preliminary expenses are covered. After that date he and the publisher divide all profits equally, so that if the book prove a success, the publisher may receive a considerable sum ; and, as he has the copyright, he will continue to receive such sum as long as the book is in demand.

Now, in order to induce the author to enter into an agreement of this kind, it is not unusual to lay before him an estimate of the cost of production, so that he may appreciate the serious " risk " the publisher is taking on his shoulders, and understand how reasonable is the demand that he should part with his copyright for ever. Sometimes this estimate is made part of the agreement which the author has to sign, it being thus, we suppose, intended to bind the author down to the prices charged in the estimate. Yet it generally happens that the actual cost of producing the book falls below this estimate. This may be due to an error in reckoning the number of sheets and the quantity of paper required ; or to such items as " author's corrections " and " advertisements," which it is clear neither party can estimate with accuracy. But in some cases—we say it with regret—prices are charged in this estimate which the publisher must know to be excessive.

Here is an instance which has come before the Society of Authors :—

Estimate

For producing 2,000 copies of "————————," to form one volume of (say) 9 sheets of 16 pages in foolscap 8vo.

	£	s.	d.
Composition, say 9 sheets at £2 4s. per sheet	19	16	o
Stereotyping, say			
Corrections, say 10 hours at 1s. per hour of work	o	10	o
Wood block and electros, 1 block at £7 10s. per block	7	10	o
Binder's blocks			
Maps			
Paper, say 36 reams at 19s. per ream	34	4	o
Plate paper for wrappers	3	16	o
Machining, say 36 reams at 6s. 6d.	11	14	o
„ wrapper	2	18	o
Binding 2,000 copies, at £2 4s. per 1,000 copies	4	8	o
Preparation of MS. for press	o	10	6
Insurance	o	6	8
Sundry Incidental Expenses....			
Advertisements (say) at scale prices	25	o	o
	£110	13	2

Should the MS., with or without additions thereto in the proofs (if any), yield more or less than the estimated number of sheets, or should it be thought advisable to increase or reduce the expenditure by way of Advertisements, then, and every such case, this Estimate will be affected *pro rata* in the items Composition, Stereotyping, Paper, Machining, Binding, and Advertisements respectively.

The estimate materially over-states the necessary expenses. The charge of £2 5s. per sheet for composition is absurd. The publisher will not have to pay this price, or anything like this price. From £1 to £1 5s. is a high price to pay. The printing again could have been done for £5 or £6 at the outside. Here is what 2,000 copies of such a book could have been produced for, the £25 for advertisement being added, and the very best paper used.

	£	s.	d.
Composition, 9 sheets at £1 5s. per sheet	11	5	o
Corrections	o	10	o
Wood-block	1	10	o
Printing, 9 sheets at 13s. per sheet	5	17	o
Binding, 2,000 in paper wrappers	6	o	o
Paper, 2,000 copies	30	o	o
Advertisement (say)	25	o	o
	£80	2	o

It is easy to imagine that an author might be willing to sign an agreement, believing the publisher's risk to be £110 13s., when he would not be so willing if he understood the risk to be only £80 2s.

It will here be instructive to notice the two accounts which follow. The first was rendered to the author upon a half-profit agreement. The second was got from an efficient and experienced printer.

1. *Publisher's Account.*

		£	s.	d.
Paper and print, 750 copies		154	4	o
Correcting (Printer's charge)		34	13	o
Drawing illustrations.... .... £42 0 0				
Drawing illustrations on stone and printing 750 sets 52 13 1				
		94	13	1
		283	10	1
Binding 500 sets, 2 vols., 65s.		34	18	9
Advertising		79	6	o
		£397	14	10

2. *Independent Printer's Estimate.*

(Containing no charges for advertisement, or "author's corrections.")

	£	s.	d.
Printing and paper	123	o	o
Drawing illustrations	30	o	o
Printing and transferring to stone	13	o	o
2 Maps	3	10	o
Lithographing maps	1	10	o
Binding....	31	5	o
	£202	5	o

Here is a difference of £85 between the publisher's account and the printer's estimate, adding the charges for advertisement and " author's corrections," exactly as they are rendered.

The accounts are particularly instructive as showing at once that the author is reasonable in believing that he is sometimes considerably overcharged. In short, if the cost of production is left to the discretion of the publisher, it will often be so high that there will be no profits to divide. If a publisher can charge what he likes for " author's corrections " and advertisement, he will often appear to the author to have charged a great deal too much, and it will be difficult in the face of proven facts to convince the author that he is wrong in any way, save by showing him the printer's bill.

Here is another Half-Profit agreement :—

" *We take all the risks of the cost of production and advertising, &c., charging the account with every item of cost of production, such as paper, composition, reasonable corrections, printing, binding, and advertising* AT THE ACTUAL COST :* *we also add an item to cover general business expenses, calculated at the rate of* 10 *per cent., when the total expenses are under* £150, *and* 7½ *per cent. when they exceed that sum. All sales are accounted for on the terms and conditions mentioned in this agreement. Should the sales not realise sufficient to cover the expenses, the deficiency is our loss : and should the proceeds of sales be in excess of the items of cost, this excess forms the profit to be equally divided.*"

And this is the agreement :—

1. The Publishers agree to print and publish at their own risk and expense the work entitled " ——————," of which the said A. B. is the author.

2. The author guarantees that the work is original and in no way whatever an infringement of any copyright belonging to any other

---

* Note the words in capitals. Is it to be inferred that other firms charge the author more than the actual cost?

person, and that it contains nothing of a libellous or scandalous character.

3. The author agrees to cede and assign to the Publishers the exclusive right, during the legal term of copyright, to publish the work, or any translation or reprint of it, in such manner as and where-soever they shall from time to time think fit, upon the following terms, namely :—

4. The cost of paper, printing, binding, advertisements, and illustrations (if any), and all other incidental expenses with reference to its publication shall be borne in the first instance by the Publishers, and shall be deducted from the money arising from sales of the work. The Publishers shall also be entitled to deduct from such moneys a further sum (to cover general business expenses) equal to £10 per cent. on their aforesaid outlay when it is under £150, and equal to £7 10s. per cent. on such outlay when it amounts to or exceeds £150.

5. The Author has contributed £50 (fifty pounds) towards the cost of production, the same to be refunded to him after the expenses have been covered by sales, and before any division of profits takes place.

6. All copies sold shall be accounted for at a reduction of one-third from the publishing price (thirteen copies to be reckoned as twelve), being the average net trade allowance, unless it shall be found desirable to dispose of any copies, or of the remainder of any copies, or of the remainder of any editions of the work, at a lower price, which price, as well as the publishing price, shall be left to the dis-cretion of the Publishers.

7. The clear profits from the sale of the work, or from the sale of the right to reprint or translate it, in this or other countries, shall be divided into two equal shares, one of which two shares shall be paid to the Author, his executors, administrators, or assigns, and the other one share shall belong to and be retained by the Publishers.

8. Accounts shall be made up and rendered half-yearly.

9. The Author agrees to pay personally all cost of corrections and alterations in the proof-sheets beyond ten shillings for every sixteen pages of print.

Note in this agreement the following points :—

(1.) The copyright is assigned to the publishers for ever. Why? As a set-off to their risk in publishing at their own expense? But they have already had £50 as such a set-off: to give away, as well and in addition, a per-manent interest in what may be a valuable property is over-generous on the author's part.

(2.) The publishers cannot in this case charge what

they like for production. They have undertaken to charge only the *actual cost* plus a certain percentage. They should, therefore, further undertake to show their books and vouchers in support of their offer. At present they could only be compelled to do so by legal process, but if they really mean what they offer, they will require no such compulsion.

It is not intended in the least to suggest that this firm would not be ready to show their books on application. I think that such an application has more than once been made to them, and has been readily granted. On the other hand the agreement contains no clause showing the author that he has a right to demand such investigation.

(3.) They have also guaranteed only to charge for advertisement the sum actually spent in this manner (plus the small percentage). This is a great point, but there is still no limit set to the advertising, and no suggestion that the publishers should be made to show vouchers in proof of their charges.*

(4.) All percentages to the publisher upon the cost of production must be vicious in a half-profit agreement. Presumably it is to the interest of both parties to keep the cost low, so that the profits to be shared may be high ; actually we see here that one party has a direct pecuniary interest in making the cost of production as high as possible.

These are not good terms for the author.

Here is another agreement, the principal feature of which is, that under it the publisher purports to bear half the expense of production.

FIRSTLY. The Publishers shall print, publish, and advertise, and sell at their own expense and risk, a first edition of 500 copies, and as many subsequent editions as they may think desirable of the work written by the Author, and entitled "——————." SUBJECT to a payment to them by the Author of the sum of £90, being about one second part of the expenses as estimated in the Schedule hereunto

---

* The question of advertisement is discussed in Chapter VII.

attached. Such payment to be made one-third on publication, and two-thirds six months after publication of the book.

SECONDLY. The Publishers shall produce the work in the best style of workmanship in three volumes on good paper, and bound' in a suitable style of binding, and shall deliver the usual press copies to the London journals, and warehouse the bound and quire stock free of charge. The Publishers shall be entitled to issue the second and following editions at lower prices.

THIRDLY. The Copyright and Plant of the work, including all Copyright, foreign, and other rights under existing or future treaties or conventions with America or other foreign counties, and the rights of translation and reproduction, and all other Imperial, Colonial, and foreign rights which now or during the continuance of the legal term of Copyright shall be, or shall become appurtenant to the proprietor of the Copyright of a book, shall be the property of the Publishers, subject to the following arrangement, that is to say, the profits accruing from the publication of the first edition of the work shall be divided between the Author and the Publishers in the ratio of their respective payments towards the cost of such first edition, as per Schedule attached. Should the Publishers desire to issue a second or subsequent edition or editions of the book, all expenses attaching thereto shall be undertaken by themselves at their own risk (unless otherwise mutually agreed), and the profits accruing therefrom shall be divided equally between the Author and themselves.

FOURTHLY. The general management of the production, publication, and sale of the work shall be left to the judgment and discretion of the Publishers, including the power of making, upon such terms as they may think advisable, or of declining arrangements with reference to the production, publication, translation, and sale of the work and translations thereof in India, the Colonies, America, and other foreign countries. The Publishers shall do their best to promote sales of the book, and in all ways treat it as though it were a publication in which their own sole interest were involved.

FIFTHLY. The expenses of the Author's proof corrections to the extent of ten pounds sterling as per Schedule shall be debited to the joint account, but should such expenses exceed this amount the Author shall refund the excess thereof to the Publishers on publication of the work.

SIXTHLY. The Publishers shall account for all sales as thirteen as twelve at two-thirds of the selling price, less a discount of ten per centum thereupon, in consideration whereof (these being the Publishers' trade "Journey Terms" upon which the greater portion only of their publications are sold) the Publishers shall make no charges for any sundry expenses of dinner, sales, journeys, commissions, bookings, telegrams, or postages, that may be incurred in the interest of sales, PROVIDED ALWAYS that should it be thought desirable to dispose of copies of the book or of the "Remainder" or a part or parts thereof at a reduced price, or by auction, whether for the American, Colonial, Indian, or other foreign market or markets, or in England, then and in every such case the net amount thus realised only shall be carried to the credit of the joint account.

SEVENTHLY. Accounts shall be made up annually by the Publishers, to Midsummer, and be rendered to the Author shortly after that time, and amounts due on such statements of account shall be settled on or before the fifteenth day of August next following, PROVIDED ALWAYS, that should the work achieve an immediate and considerable financial success, the Publishers shall, six months after publication of the work, if so desired by the Author, make an approximate cash advance of one-half of the Author's profits, in view of their prospective statement of account. The Publishers shall, however, render to the Author a first statement of account six months after publication of the book, and the amount due to the Author if any, on such statement, shall be deducted from the amount due by the Author to the Publishers at this date as per clause FIRSTLY hereabove.

Estimate

For producing 500 copies of "————————," to form 3 volumes of (say) 46 sheets of 16 pages in crown 8vo. Long Primer (O.S.)

	£	s.	d.
Composition, say 46 sheets at £1 16s. per sheet	82	16	0
Stereotyping, say at per sheet			
Corrections, say 200 hours at per hour of work	10	0	
Wood blocks and electros, blocks at per block			
,, ,, ,, ,, ...	1	2	6
,, ,, ,, ,, ...			
Binder's blocks			
Maps, maps at per map			
Paper, say 46 reams at 19s. per ream	43	14	0
Plate paper, reams at ,, ...			
Machining, say 46 reams at 9s. per ream	20	14	0
,, wood blocks			
Binding, 200 copies at £75 per 1,000 copies	15	0	0
Preparation of MS. for press	1	1	0
Publisher's Reader	2	2	0
Insurance	0	16	8
Sundry Incidental Expenses....			
Advertisements, say at scale prices	30	0	0
	£207	6	2

Should the MS., with or without additions thereto in the proofs (if any), yield more or less than the estimated number of sheets, or should it be thought advisable to increase or reduce the expenditure by way of Advertisements, then and in every such case this Estimate will be affected *pro rata* in the items of Composition, Stereotyping, Paper, Machining, and Binding, and Advertisements respectively.

(Signed)

The points to be noted are :—

(1.) The author is called upon to cede his copyright. Now in the first half-profit agreement that we quoted we took reasonable exception to such a proceeding, but there the publisher was producing the work at his own risk. Here he is not, and the demand of the copyright is scandalous.

(2.) The author is asked to pay £90 as "being about one-second part of the expenses" of production. As a matter of fact £90 represents a much larger proportion of the expenses. The author did not know this, or he would never have consented to pay £90. The real cost of production of 500 copies of a 3 vol. novel, of 46 sheets of sixteen pages, in crown 8vo., Long Primer, Old Style, is only £97, thus :—

	£	s.	d.
Composition, 46 sheets at £1 4s. per sheet....	55	4	0
Printing, 46 sheets at 5s. per sheet	11	10	0
Binding 200 copies	11	0	0
Paper	20	0	0
	97	14	0
Add for advertisement	30	0	0
	£127	14	0

The publishers' real risk is therefore under £10, exclusive of advertising, the author having paid £90.

(3.) Again the estimate is based upon the theory that the book will form 46 sheets. Suppose it is not so large a book, it is evident that by as much as the guess at its size has been too big, by so much will the total estimated risk be swollen, and by so much will the author's payment of

£90 appear reasonable. Such slips in these estimates have occurred.

(4.) Under the fourth clause of the agreement, advertisement would be left solely to the discretion of the publisher. Now the author has a direct interest in keeping the advertisement charges low ; he ought to be allowed some chance of doing so. Bearing in mind the fact that over-charges in advertisement have before now been made, there ought to be a stipulation in the agreement that the author shall be at liberty to assure himself, in the only way possible, that the amount so debited against the book has been really spent.

These are not good terms for the author.

The following is a half-profit agreement which much more nearly realises the ordinary idea of a just business contract. There is not much fault to be found with it.

FIRSTLY. The said C. D. shall publish at their own expense and risk, "—————" A. B.'s work.

SECONDLY. After deducting from the produce of the sale of the said work the expenses of production and publication thereof, the profits remaining of every edition that may be printed, or translations thereof, and the receipts from every source on account of the said work, arising from the publication, reproduction abroad, translation, and sale thereof during the legal term of Copyright, shall be divided into two equal parts : one moiety to be paid to the said A. B., and the other moiety to belong to C. D. and Co., it being expressly agreed that no profits shall be accounted as made until the said C. D. shall have been reimbursed all the said expenses.

THIRDLY. The expenses of production shall be taken to mean the actual sums paid by C. D. for printing, paper, binding, engraving, and advertising, and also for any incidental expenditure incurred in the production of the work, it being expressly understood that any discounts received by C. D. for cash payments or otherwise shall be brought into account and credited to the work.

FOURTHLY. The expenses of publication, viz., rent, rates, and taxes of offices, clerks, travellers, warehousemen, porters, insurance, bad debts, &c., shall be fixed at 10 per cent. on the gross produce of the work.

FIFTHLY. Corrections above ten shillings per sheet of   pages (on the average) to be charged to the said A. B., and deducted from his share of the profits.

SIXTHLY. The books to be accounted for at the trade sale. Price 25 as 24, or 13 as 12 (with a deduction of 5 per cent. to cover trade discounts), unless it be thought advisable at any time to dispose of copies of the remainder at a lower price, which is left to the judgment and discretion of C. D. Any extra discounts for cash payments, export orders, or otherwise which C. D. may deem it advisable to allow to the trade, shall be brought into account and debited against the work.

SEVENTHLY. The Copyright in the work and the translations thereof, including all Copyright, foreign, and other rights under existing or future treaties or conventions with America and other foreign countries, and under the Canadian Copyright Act, 1875, and any other present or future Indian or Colonial, and all rights of translation and reproduction, and all other Imperial, Colonial, and foreign rights, which now, or during the continuance of the legal term of Copyright, shall be or become appurtenant to the proprietor of the Copyright or the work, shall be the joint property of A. B. and C. D. in equal shares ; one moiety shall belong to the said A. B., and the other moiety to the said C. D.

EIGHTHLY. The general management of the production, publication, and sale of the work shall be left to the judgment and discretion of C. D., including the power of making, on such terms as they may think advisable (or of declining), arrangements with reference to the reproduction, publication, translation, and sale of the work, and translations thereof.

These are the points that should be observed :—

(1.) The publishers undertake to charge the work with only the *actual* cost of production, crediting the author with any discounts they may receive. This is a distinct advance. It remains for a clause to be added, wherein it shall be provided that the proof that the alleged charges have been incurred shall be properly furnished if required, as a matter of course, to any accountant sent by the author for the purpose. I have no doubt that if an author's demand appeared reasonable, every facility would be given him by the firm to investigate their joint accounts : but why not put it in the agreement ? If such a firm as this, and some half-a-dozen others, would print such an offer on their forms, some enterprising people well known to the Society of Authors would cease to carry on business.

(2.) Joint possession of the copyright for subsequent editions is not a good plan. It merits praise when compared with the total surrender exacted by the previous agreements, but it is really not a much better arrangement. While author and publisher are satisfied with each other it does not matter really who has the copyright, but we have to consider a possible disagreement. If such should occur in this case the book would be killed. The author would not sanction the issue of further editions from the original firm, the publisher would not allow a new firm to publish the work.

(3.) Clause (8) provides that the publishers should have entire discretion as to the production, inclusive, of course, of advertisement. Now, as the author does not receive his money till the cost of production is covered, he is interested in keeping the expenses of advertisement down, and ought to have a voice in the matter. The agreement should provide that not more than a certain sum should be spent in this manner without his leave, and that vouchers should be forthcoming in verification.

The last form of publishing upon this system, of which an example will be given, is that which it is proposed to call the "*Half-profit Dodge*."

The following letter constitutes the agreement as proposed, and as almost invariably entered upon. In literally dozens of cases that have come before the Society this letter has never varied, save in the magnitude of the sums that the "Dodger" proposes to receive. In every case the sequence of events that has brought the author to us has been the same. Yet we note sorrowfully that, in spite of repeated exposure, this method of half-profit "publishing" still exists :—

We hereby agree to produce this work in one shilling volume form, good paper and type being used, on your undertaking to pay us the sum of £22 10s. in the following manner :—Two-thirds (£15) on our going to press, and the balance £7 10s. on your seeing the last proofs. We further agree to meet all demands for sales up to five thousand copies for a first edition, to advertise the book prior to

D

the day of issue, and to produce the book before the   inst.
Profits to be equally divided between author and publisher. Accounts
of sales to be rendered once in every three months.

(Signed)   The Publisher.
The Author.

This is what always happens.

First, a large bill is sent in for "author's corrections."

Next, the author is told that his book will not "go" without full advertisement, and is requested to send a cheque for the same at once. If he smells a rat, and is slow with his cheque, it is probable that he may have some difficulty in getting his book issued, though it is generally all printed, so that the man may secure what he calls in his letter his "balance." It may be noted that, in the example we have given, the publisher offered to advertise the book prior to the day of issue. This is an unusual offer, but what does it amount to? The expenditure of 3s. will enable him to technically fulfil this offer, when he is able to demand from the author a cheque for all future advertisement.

Then the author gets no accounts, and on writing to know why, is told that there have been no sales. Of course there have been no sales : in many instances, the book is so poor that this is not to be wondered at ; but however good it were, people of this publisher's sort could not sell it.

By this time the author is suspicious.

He takes advice and finds first that the £22 10s. which he paid as the half cost of 5,000 copies, is more than double the cost of 250 copies, got up in the wretched manner these productions always are. But he learns that an edition of 250 copies is probably all that have been produced. Yet he cannot make the man print more than 250 copies, though he has been paid nominally for 5,000, for lo! the publisher has not engaged to print that 5,000 copies, but only to meet demands up to that number. In addition, the author has generally paid sums for advertisement and for "author's corrections" which he now feels were sheer extortion.

These kind of people tout for business and advertise

for clients. Whatever MSS. are submitted to them their reader will always report *favourably* upon them, for on every printing transaction the firm makes a certain sum of money.

Here is what a well-known London journal has to say upon the subject :—

"To sum up, the essence of the thing consists in furnishing an estimate (a more or less accurate estimate so as to afford *primâ facie* evidence of strict integrity if the victim *should* have the curiosity to enquire into the figures for himself) for an enormous edition and then to produce just as few copies as the customs of the trade permit. The peculiar mischief of it is, that so far from the publisher risking a half share of the cost of production, he risks not one farthing. He works solely upon the author's capital. Not only that, but he has a handsome profit assured before he goes to press, even though the book should perish still-born ; while if by chance the work makes a hit, his profits increase proportionately. It matters, therefore, not one whit to him what rubbish he gets hold of. The one thing needful is the author's contribution. Consequently any fool who has learned to hold a pen, and can raise the requisite cash, is at his mercy. I beseech every amateur author to bethink him of this when the next half-profit publisher offers him fame and fortune at the ridiculously low figure of £22 10s."

This is not the place to seriously discuss the methods of these people. The author's money not the public's monies is their aim. Occasionally the law is able to interfere with it. But always a law court is the place where the discussion should take place.

Remember, however, that their actions are only possible :—

(1.) Because the indignant objection of certain supposed reputable firms to giving vouchers allows rogues to hide behind the formula, "custom of the trade," when refusing to account for the alleged cost : (2) Because the young author will rush into publication without advice.

It has been said—but it is said no longer by the

best houses—that a demand for vouchers and the auditing
of accounts is a reflection on the publisher's personal honesty.
This, of course, is not the case.   The position really is
this—it can be proved that over and over again unscrupulous publishers, protected by the custom of not
producing receipts, have made very large secret profits,
by overcharging items of production, and dealing with
advertisement by methods we shall presently discuss.   In
the face of this fact no half-profit arrangement can
escape condemnation, unless clauses in the agreement
secure to the author *proof* that he has received half the
profits.   In every joint-undertaking in every other business,
wherever men have profits to share, or charges to make,
they furnish such proof.   Why not in publishing?   The
secretary of a society has his balance sheet audited—does
he cry out that the ceremony reflects on his personal
honour?   The chairman of a company sends his yearly
statements to professional auditors—does he cry out that
he is offended and insulted by the necessity? and what
would the public say if he did so cry out?

Next, what have the publishers done for a book that
they should absorb half the profits?   The fact of their
publishing a book does not make it popular.   The half-
profit system, when based upon the fairest agreement, can
only be recommended in cases where the sale is certain to
be so limited that the publisher, by an honest "half-profit"
charge, gets no more than a reasonable return for his
time and trouble.   For a successful author to give a
publisher half-profits is madness, while it is not much
better than madness for any author to enter into a per-
manent arrangement, whereby half the profits of a possibly
valuable property become lost to him.

In view of the facts that the assignment of the copyright
is almost *always* demanded by the publisher, and that the
author almost *never* receives a half of the profits :—

   *Is the method of "half-profit," in any of its forms, a
satisfactory one to writers ?*

As varieties of the half-profit system, it is occasionally

suggested that the profits should be divided into thirds or fourths, and the publisher's fraction is frequently the larger.

There has been nothing said about the half-profit system, which is not applicable to these methods. Whatever fraction the author is to receive, he can never know that he receives it, because he never knows what the initial cost has been. He only knows what his bill says.

The Society of Authors has before it now a case where a lady paid, as one-third of the cost of production, £55. The real cost of the whole book was £40.

In another case the author paid £35 as half the cost of production, in return for which he was to receive three-fifths of the profits. The real cost of production turned out to have been £24.

In another case the author was to receive half-profits after 700 copies had been sold. Only 750 copies were ever printed, and of these the usual quantity were sent to the press. Certainly the publisher paid the cost of production, but equally certainly the author wrote the book and could never make anything by it.

In another case the author paid £50 to the publisher, and was to receive in return one-third of the profits.

The agreement enacted that the author should take one-third of the profits, and that the publishers should publish at their own risk and expense, after his payment of £50, they taking the copyright.

Copies sold were to be accounted for at a one-third reduction from the publishing price, and the clear profits were to be divided into three equal shares—one share to belong to the author, and two shares to the publisher.

Accounts were to be made up half yearly.

The author was to pay all cost of corrections beyond 5s. for every 16 pages.

The publisher was allowed to charge £21 for revising and other expenses.

After the sale of the first edition the profits were to be divided equally between author and publisher; if future editions were called for.

The account, being curious, is subjoined.

Expenditure.

	£	s.	d.
To Engraving or transferring ditto	8	17	1
„ Paper	38	9	3
Plate paper for illustrations.			
„ Composing, printing, and pressing 3,000 copies....	55	11	3
„ illustrations.			
„ prospectuses, &c.			
Moulding, stereotyping, and electrotyping.			
„ Binding	12	13	0
„ Advertisements	34	18	0
Law charges.			
Bad debts.			
Office and warehouse expenses.			
„ Carriage and postage	5	19	2
„ Charges, viz., goods	0	3	7
„ Trade discounts, 40 per cent.	22	1	1
„ Reader's honorarium as per agreement	21	0	0
Surplus at this date.			
	£199	12	5

Cr.

Receipts.

	£	s.	d.
By Cash	50	0	0
Including sales to author or proprietor, also			
copies sold at a reduced price.			
Authorizations.			
Town sales — copies netting.			
County „ „			
Foreign and } „			
Colonial sales }			
Agents „ „			
Cash „ „			
Annual } „ „			
Dinner }			
Copies sold, , in cloths and sheets.			
„ 775 C. 2s. = 59 doz. 13/12 and 8/7½ at 17s.	50	13	8
„ 62 C. 2s. 6d. = 4 „ „ 10/9½ at 21s.	5	0	7
„ 18 C. 3s. 6d. = 1 „ „ 5/4½ at 30s.	2	1	3
Deficiency at this date	91	16	11
	£199	12	5

Is it wonderful that there is a deficiency when the publisher takes such discounts? If the whole edition printed were sold there would still be a deficiency.

To denounce the half-profit system may seem to be killing a dead horse, this universally discredited method having dropped into dishonoured oblivion.

On this, two things may be said :

(1.) Some of the documents quoted in this Chapter bear quite a recent date. There are several well-known houses who do publish still on this method, though the really first-rate firms no longer do so. The snake is scotched, not killed.

(2.) The Society of Authors from the beginning clamoured against the half-profit system, as generally understood, declaring it to hold out direct inducements to fraud. Then—some five years ago—certain firms called the Society cantankerous and unreasonable in their clamour. And now the system is universally discredited. At least the Society is so informed.

CHAPTER V.

IV.—THE ROYALTY SYSTEM.

THE method of payment by royalty, when proposed, was eagerly welcomed by the majority of authors as a plan by which they would get something at least, while it also appeared to them to offer the great inducement of a return in proportion to the sales. As yet it had not occurred to any author to ask what was his just share of profits, and what, therefore, should be his royalty. He was satisfied to think that he would "get something," and that the larger the sale the more he would get.

The royalty system has, therefore, been widely adopted; we shall see how far it has deserved its popularity.

There are three methods chiefly employed. They are :—

(1.) The publisher brings out the book at his own cost and offers the author a fixed royalty from the beginning.

(2.) The publisher produces the work at his own cost, and offers the author a royalty on every copy sold over and above a certain number.

(3.) The publisher produces the work at his own cost and offers the author a royalty on every copy sold, after the cost of production has been recovered.

It is proposed to give examples, one or more, of each method, with the agreements, and so show how the system, on each of its most usual methods, works from the author's point of view.

(1.) *Where the publisher produces the work at his own cost, and offers the author a fixed royalty from the beginning.*

Here is an agreement upon these lines :—

FIRSTLY. The Publishers shall print, publish, advertise, and sell, at their own expense and risk, a new edition, and as many subsequent editions as they may think desirable, of the work written by the Author, entitled "——————."

SECONDLY. The Publishers shall produce the work in the best style of workmanship, in one volume, on good paper, and bound in a suitable style of binding.

THIRDLY. The Copyright of the work, including all Copyright foreign and other rights under existing or future treaties or conventions, with America, or other foreign countries, shall be the property of the Publishers, SUBJECT to the payment by them to the Author of a Royalty of ten per centum on the first thousand, and ten per centum on all following copies sold, sales being calculated thirteen as twelve, and such Royalty being allowed upon the nominal or selling price of the book. AND SUBJECT further to a Royalty of fifty per centum on all monies received by them for the rights of translation or reproduction, PROVIDED ALWAYS that should it be thought desirable to dispose of copies of the work, or of the "Remainder," or a part or parts thereof, at a reduced price, (which is left to the judgment and discretion of the Publishers,) then, and in every such case, the Royalty to be paid to the Author in respect of such sales shall be five per centum on the net amount thus realised, in lieu of the full Royalty due upon copies sold at the regular trade price.

FOURTHLY. The general management of the production, publication, and sale of the work shall be left to the judgment and discretion of the Publishers, including the power of making, upon such terms as they may think advisable, or of declining arrangements with reference to the production, publication, translation, and sale of the work, and translations thereof, in India, and the Colonies, America and other foreign countries.

FIFTHLY. The Publishers shall undertake the expenses of the author's proof corrections to the extent of SIX pounds sterling, but should such expenses exceed this amount the Author shall refund such balance to the Publishers on Publication of the work.

SIXTHLY. Accounts shall be made up annually by the Publishers.

It is immaterial whether it is proposed to issue the book at the nominal price of 6s. or at the nominal price of 3s. 6d. (the second clause states that the book is to be produced in one volume, and these are the two most usual prices). Let us select the former figure and consider the respective positions of the contracting parties if the book meets with success.

The cost of production of 1,000 copies of a 6s. novel, inclusive of moulding, stereotyping, and advertisement (£20) is £95 (a liberal estimate). If then the whole edition of 1,0co copies, sold on the terms mentioned in the third clause of this agreement, "trade price," the profits would be £90, and the royalties due to the author £30.

Hence on the first edition of the work the publishers would be over £30 out of pocket.*

But 3,000 more copies can be produced for £120, all the processes being cheaper for a large quantity, no moulding and stereotyping and less advertisement being also required. The profits upon their sale would be at least £400, whereof the author would receive under £100 and the publisher the rest, and the more successful the book is, the more glaringly unfair becomes the division of profits.

The author publishing a successful book upon such principles may well be sore at the results to himself. For an initial risk of £95, upon security which he has considered sufficient, the publisher obtains this enormous and increasing share of the profits, and obtains it permanently.

The following account was rendered to an author, and the figures illustrate well the ascending scale of the

---

* It will, in this Chapter, often be necessary to allude to the cost of production of a novel, and to the sums that should be realised by its sales. The following are two independent estimates for the production of two different novels rendered by two well-known printers.

Estimate for 1,000 copies of a 6s. novel of average length :—

							£	s.	d.
Composition	...	...	...	...	...	...	20	8	0
Printing	...	...	...	...	...	...	7	13	0
Paper	...	...	...	...	...	...	15	10	0
Binding	...	...	...	...	...	...	17	13	0
Moulding	...	...	...	...	...	...	4	5	0
Stereotyping	...	...	...	...	...	...	7	13	0
Advertising	...	...	...	...	...	...	20	0	0
							£93	2	0

Estimate for a 6s. novel—1,000 copies :—

							£	s.	d.
Composition	...	...	...	...	...	...	26	0	0
Printing	...	...	...	...	...	...	9	0	0
Paper	...	...	...	...	...	...	15	3	0
Binding	...	...	...	...	...	...	15	0	0
Moulding	...	...	...	...	...	...	5	0	0
Stereotyping	...	...	...	...	...	...	9	0	0
Advertising	...	...	...	...	...	...	20	0	0
							£99	3	0

It will be seen at once that in detail they do not quite correspond with each other, although, as a whole, they agree very well. The larger novel was on inferior paper, and not quite so well bound as the other.

With regard to the sum that would be realised by sales, the trade price of a 6s. book is very generally 3s. 8d., and this sum multiplied by 1,000 is £183 6s. 8d. A few copies have to be sold at specially reduced prices, but a few copies may also be sold at the full price.

A 10 per cent. royalty upon 1,000 copies sold at 6s. each is £30.

publisher's profits under this system. The agreement was that the author should receive a royalty of 15 per centum on every copy sold. The first edition consisted of 750 copies, and that number will be sufficient for our case.

Publication Account.

188	£	s.	d.	£	s.	d.
To Paper, 22½ reams at 20s. 7d.	....		....	23	3	2
„ Printing 750 copies—						
Composing 14⅞ sheets....	46	2	3			
Extra for Bourgeois	0	5	0			
Author's corrections and cancelled matter....	106	13	0			
Nightwork	2	5	0			
Working, at 15 sheets = 22½ reams at 13s....	14	12	6			
Cold pressing	1	2	6			
Specimens	1	9	0			
				172	9	3
„ Binding 600 at £4 4s.				26	8	0
„ Advertising....				71	14	8
„ Incidental expenses				15	3	0
„ Royalty to Author on sales (495 copies at 24s., £594)				89	2	0
„ Honorarium agreed upon by Author for assistance				25	0	0
„ Balance forward				7	3	5
				£430	3	6

188				£	s.	d.	£	s.	d.
By Amount charged to A. B. for corrections							91	15	6
750 Printed—									
150 Quires } on hand									
60 Cloth }									
6 British Museum.									
34 Review, gratis.									
6 Author.									
255 —									
„ Sales 495									
150 as 144 Mudie at 12s.							86	8	0
345 as 319		255	4	0					
495 Discount 5 per cent. allowed off 80		3	4	0					
							252	0	c
							£430	3	6
By Balance forward (C. D. and Co.'s profit) ...							£7	3	5

This, then, is the position:—on a sale of the first 500 copies the author loses money. He pays £91 15*s.* 6*d.* for "corrections" and cancelled matter, and receives £89 2*s.* as royalty.

Loss £2 13*s.* 6*d.*

The publisher, on the other hand, has to pay £331 4*s.* 7*d.** to produce 750 copies, and receives £338 8*s.* 0*d.* by sales of 500.

Gain £7 3*s.* 5*d.*

If the other 200 copies are sold (allowing 50 for press-copies) the publisher will make £89 4*s.* 7*d.* by the sales, and the author will make £36 by royalties; so that on the whole edition—taking the publisher's own figures—the author will make £33 17*s.* 6*d.* and the publisher just 8*s.* under £100.

Of course as more copies are sold the position of affairs gets worse for the author; while the publisher's situation will really be better than we have given him credit for, if his initial expenses were not so heavy as is alleged in the account.

These are not good results for the author.

(2.) *Where the publisher produces the work at his own cost, and offers the author a royalty on every copy sold over and above a certain number.*

A specimen agreement:—

FIRSTLY. The Publishers shall print, publish, advertise, and sell at their own expense and risk, a first edition and as many subsequent

---

* (1) Composition £3 2*s.* a sheet. This is very high.

(2) Advertisement £71 14*s.* 8*d.* Of course a large sum like this ought to be accounted for in detail. Vouchers, or at any rate explanation, would doubtless be forthcoming, but a clause in the agreement giving the author the right to demand proofs, must be the only satisfactory arrangement.

(3) "Incidental Expenses." What?

(4) "Author's Corrections and Cancelled Matter." The publisher states that he has been at an expense of £106 13*s.* in this item. That is to say, that the "corrections" and cancelling amount to more than double the original cost of composition. It is fair to allow, first that a reduction was made, and second, that there were reasons why the corrections were unusually heavy.

editions as they may think desirable, of the work written by the Author, and entitled provisionally "————————."

SECONDLY. The Publishers shall produce the work in three or four volumes, and shall deliver the usual press copies to the London and provincial journals. Bad debts shall be their charge, and books thus unpaid for shall be subject to Royalties to the Author.

THIRDLY. The Copyright of the work, and the rights of translation and reproduction, and all other Imperial, Colonial, and Foreign rights, which now or during the continuance of the legal term of Copyright shall be or shall become appurtenant to the proprietor of the Copyright of a book shall be the property of the Publishers, SUBJECT to the payment by them to the Author of a Royalty of nil per centum on the first thousand copies sold, and 15 per centum on all following copies sold, sales being calculated 13 as 12, and such Royalty being payable on the trade price, which shall be taken at two-thirds of the nominal or published price, PROVIDED ALWAYS that should it be thought desirable to dispose of copies of the work or of the " Remainder," or a part or parts thereof, at a reduced price (which is left to the judgment and discretion of the Publishers), then and in every case the Royalty payable to the Author in respect of such sales shall be 5 per centum on the nett amount thus realised, in lieu of the full Royalty due upon copies sold at the regular trade price.

FOURTHLY. The general management of the production, publication, and sale of the work shall be left to the judgment and discretion of the Publishers, including the power of making, upon such terms as they may think advisable, or of declining, arrangements with reference to the production, publication, translation, and sale of the work and translations thereof, in India, the Colonies, America, and other foreign countries. The Publishers shall do their best to promote sales of the book, and in all ways treat it as though it were a publication in which their own sole interest were involved.

FIFTHLY. The expenses of the Author's proof corrections to the extent of £3 sterling shall be the charge of the Publishers, but should such expenses exceed this amount the balance shall be debited to the Author's account with the Publishers.

This document will be discussed generally, while its bearings are pointed out as as a royalty agreement.

(1.) The author assigns the copyright entirely to the publishers. Why? Do they buy it? They do not even pay royalties until a large number of copies have been sold. It would seem as if the author, not content with a miserably low royalty, had suddenly thought that it would be only fair to present the publishers with all his right in a property whose value he did not know.

(2.) He is to get in return—after 1,000 copies are sold —a royalty of 15 per cent. on the *trade price.* In the last agreement, the author was offered 15 per cent. on the nominal price—here he is offered 15 per cent. on the trade price. That is to say, he is to get 9 per cent. on the nominal price—and that *after* the sale of 1,000 copies. These are the figures :—

Taking as an example a six shilling book, and allowing £20 for advertisement we find that it would cost the publishers £95 at the outside to produce an edition of 1,000 copies. Their sales would realise a profit of £90. This belongs to the publisher. [*Vide* footnote to p. 58.]

If 3,000 more copies were sold the author would obtain something under £70, and the publisher something over £350. And the larger the sale the more out of all reasonable proportion would the division of profits become.

(3.) It does not appear from clause 3 that the author is to get any return from the foreign markets whose possibilities are dangled before his eyes. The royalty is to be paid upon sales of copies and not upon sales of the rights of reproduction or of the rights of translation.

(4.) Why is the author to receive a diminished royalty on " Remainder Sales "? *

(5.) Lastly and chiefly, the author is not to receive any remuneration until 1,000 copies are sold. How is he to know when this happy result is attained? By the publisher's simple statement. There is no clause in the agreement giving him a right to find out by the publisher's books, or the publisher's stock, the number of copies that have been sold. Nor has he the right to ascertain how many copies the printer has supplied. He must fall back on this statement. But an unproven statement is a guarantee that in all other commercial transactions would be laughed at. Why should it not be equally ridiculous in publishing transactions? Rather it *is* equally ridiculous. Why should it not be treated as such?

---

* *Vide* Chapter X.

The agreement is a bad one in every way for the author.

Here is another agreement, a more unfair one still, based on the same principles of royalty.

FIRSTLY. A. B. has written a work entitled "——————————," which he hereby assigns to Messrs. C. D. & Co., who agree in consideration thereof to print and publish the same in the first instance as a six shilling book, and after the sale in England of 500 (five hundred) copies to pay to A. B. a Royalty of ten per cent. on the selling price of all copies that may be sold.

SECONDLY. All details of the publication, the form and price of the book, shall be left to C. D. & Co., who shall have power to dispose of any copy or copies of the book at a lower price than that at which it was originally published if at any time they should deem it advisable to do so. Messrs. C. D. & Co. are to make the best arrangements they can for the publication of the book in the United States of America, and until such time as the 500 (five hundred) copies aforesaid of the book shall have been sold in England, the proceeds from the American sales are to be received by Messrs. C. D. & Co. and placed to the credit of the work.

THIRDLY. After the 500 (five hundred) copies heretofore referred to have been sold in England, the subsequent proceeds from the American sales are to be equally divided between Messrs. C. D. & Co. and A. B.

FOURTHLY. It is further agreed that if, at the end of one year from the publication of the book, the 500 (five hundred) copies aforesaid shall not have been sold in England, A. B. shall make good any loss there may be on account of the publication of the book.

FIFTHLY. Accounts to be made up to the 30th day of June in each year, rendered in September, and any sums due paid in the month of October following.

Note here :—

(1.) There is an absolute assignment of the copyright to the publisher. This assignment is none the less absolute because it is not mentioned in so many words. As long as the publisher pays the stipulated royalty he can produce as many editions of the book as he chooses. What is that but an assignment of copyright? In the previous cases the publisher at any rate had his risk to plead, here, (*vide* clause 4 of the agreement) there is no risk.

(2.) After the sale of 500 copies of a 6*s.* book the author is to receive 10 per cent. on the selling price. As before, how is the author to know when 500 copies have been sold? Is he to take the publisher's word?

(3.) The royalty offered would lead to the following division of profits.

By the sale of the first 500 copies the publisher would make about £5. He then has the copyright of a work that has been moulded and stereotyped entirely at his disposal.

The author obtains nothing.

From this time forward the author receives £16 on every 1,000 copies sold, and the publisher £140, of which from £80 to £90 is clear profit.

Yet this is a division of profits in a transaction where the risk is being borne by the author!

(4.) The author is to make up any loss that there may be on account of the publication of the book. How can he, when he does not know how much the publication of the book will cost? No facilities, such as permission to see the printer's bill, are placed in his way. This is, however, a question that will be treated fully under the next method of offering a royalty.

If it be asked why authors sign such agreements, the only answer is that they do not understand what they mean, and they are too anxious to get their works published at any price, to take time for consultation.

Moreover, many lawyers appear too often to be profoundly ignorant of such matters, and cannot therefore advise.

(3.) *Where the publisher produces the work at his own cost, and offers the author a royalty on every copy sold after the cost of production has been recovered.*

A specimen agreement :—

A. B. has assigned the publication of a work entitled "————" to C. D. & Co., who agree to undertake all the expenses of printing, publishing, and advertising an edition of 1,000 copies to sell at 10s. 6d., and after the sale of 450 copies nett, 13 as 12, to pay A. B. a Royalty of 3s. 6d. a copy on all copies sold nett, 13 as 12.

Type to be kept standing for 6 months, and should further editions be printed, the same Royalty to be paid, after the expenses are defrayed.

Any profits which may be realised from foreign right of translation or reproduction, or from the sale of early sheets or stereotype plates of the said work to America shall be divided equally between Author and Publisher.

The general management of the production, publication, advertising, re-printing, and sale of the work shall be left to the judgment and discretion of C. D. & Co., including the power of making, on such terms as they may think advisable, or of declining arrangements with reference to the production, publication, translation and sale of the work in India, the Colonies, America, and other foreign countries.

Should the cost of corrections, other than printer's errors, exceed on the average the sum of ten shillings per sheet of sixteen pages, such excess to be deducted from the Royalties that may become due to the said A. B.

Should the selling price of the book be increased or reduced, the Royalty to be increased or reduced *pro rata*.

(1.) It must be again pointed out that we have here the blind and reckless assignment to the publisher of what may prove to be a valuable property. So flagrant is the folly of this proceeding, that no excuse is made for monotonously returning to it.

(2.) The royalty is offered after 450 copies have been sold, but there is no clause providing for such an investigation as would be necessary to prove that no more than this number had been sold, without the author's knowledge.

(3.) But this is the chief point of interest in the agreement. The royalty is to be paid upon subsequent editions after the publisher's expenses have been defrayed. These expenses are, by the second clause, left entirely in the publisher's hands. How is the author to know what the expenses of production are? Is he—as he is expected to do in the matter of the number of sales alleged—to take the publisher's word?

Here the author is face to face with that bugbear of our Society—the *stated* cost of production. Indirectly it has already cropped up in publishing by the royalty system, and it must crop up in all publishing transactions,

E

since it is the extent of the publisher's risk that regulates the prices he offers ; but here the cost of production is the essence of the proposal, for the author is not to receive his royalty till the publisher is reimbursed. The author must be placed in a position to *know* when this point has been reached.

The agreement, like the previous ones, would be a foolish one for an author to enter upon.

Under it, the publisher, if dishonest, can debit the author's account with as large a sum as he likes, and as he has no need to prove the charges, he never need pay any royalty, unless his conscience should move him.

Again, if the publishers treated him fairly, rendered accurate accounts, and did their best to keep the cost of production low, the author would still have made a bad pecuniary bargain. The cost of production of 1,000 copies would be about £110, allowing for the cost of advertisement (£20), moulding, and stereotyping. The trade price of a half-guinea book is 6s. Therefore, without taking into consideration copies that have been disposed of at the nominal or some higher price, the publisher would receive by the sale of the first 450 copies £135 ; that is, before the author can receive anything at all, the publisher has gained £25.

Assuming that the odd 50 copies have been used for distribution to the press, there now remain 500 copies to be disposed of. These would realise £150, of which £87 10s. would go to the author and £62 10s. to the publisher. The total result on the sale of the first edition would therefore be a genuine half-profit division.

But subsequent editions of 1,000 copies can be produced for something between £80 and £90, as the expenses of moulding and stereotyping have not again to be met, nor should advertisement be any longer so heavy an item.

Take the larger figure.

The sale of 300 copies will realise thus £90, and at this point the author should begin to receive his royalty.

If he does, the arrangement is as before a genuine half-profit one, and we do not allow that the publisher is entitled to half the profits of a book.

Lastly, not only would the publisher gain most fraudulently (if he were on fraud inclined) by rendering fictitious accounts, but he would gain in what he would probably consider a legitimate manner by taking 10 per cent. on the cost of production. That is, he would gain by making that cost as heavy as possible in reality, though he might repudiate all idea of magnifying it on paper.

These considerations prevailed with the author, who withdrew from the transaction.

The following table shows at a glance the real meaning of the royalty system when honestly worked. A 6s. novel is taken as an example, and the results are calculated on proposals between 5 and 30 per cent.

It must be remembered that it costs under £100 to produce an edition of 1,000 copies of such a book, inclusive of the expense of moulding, stereotyping, and advertisement (£25).

The trade price, that is the average price actually obtained by the publisher, is not less than 3s. 6d.* a copy, so that at the least the edition realises £175. The royalties are throughout calculated on the nominal price of 6s., as it is usual to calculate them on the larger price.†

The initial expense of £100 has been deducted from the publisher's figures.

A royalty of 5 per cent. is, it must be owned, an unusually low offer, but I have seen it made, and quite lately. A royalty of 30 per cent. is, equally or more unusually, a good offer.

---

* A good many odd copies bring him in the whole 6s., while 3s. 6d. is really a little below the nominal price.

† When an author is offered a larger royalty than usual, he is advised to see on which price the offer is made.

E 2

I. On the sale of the first 1,000.

	Per cent.					
	5	10	15	20	25	30
Publisher	£ 60	£ 45	£ 30	£ 15	£ —	£ —
Author	15	30	45	60	75	90

II. On the sale of the next 3,000.

	Per cent.						
	5	10	15	20	25	30	35
Publisher ...	£ 330	£ 285	£ 240	£ 195	£ 150	£ 105	£ 60
Author	45	90	135	180	225	270	315

III. On the sale of an edition of 10,000.

	Per cent.						
	5	10	15	20	25	30	35
Publisher	£ 1,200	£ 1,050	£ 900	£ 750	£ 600	£ 450	£ 300
Author	150	300	450	600	750	900	1,050

Aided by this table it is easy to come to the broad conclusions with regard to the royalty system, but before pointing them out, I should like to anticipate a possible objection. It may be said, " But the table is calculated on the complete sale of the edition, no account being taken of the large number of cases where the issue is not so fortunate."

The table is meant to illustrate the results obtained under the royalty system by the authors of books which sell, and to show how the profits, under the usual proposals, are too often most unfairly divided.

Any publisher may occasionally make a mistake, but if a publisher *habitually* issues editions much larger than the public require, can he be thought to be a good publisher? Whose fault is it if he suffers?

(1.) No author should sign an agreement, whereby he binds himself to receive a low royalty for an indefinite number of editions.

This is equivalent to saying that he should retain his copyright, and so give himself the opportunity of reaping the rewards of any big success, by securing for himself a higher percentage of the results.

(2.) No author should sign an agreement whereby he is not to receive a royalty until a certain number of copies have been sold, unless the agreement provides facilities for the verification of the publisher's account.

(3.) No author should sign an agreement whereby he is not to receive a royalty until the cost of production is covered, unless he has every opportunity of satisfying himself that no more than the actual cost is charged.

Concerning both these latter arrangements all must admit that it is just that the author should in many cases not be paid, or be paid on a low scale, until the publisher is reimbursed. That follows upon the table.

But it is right that the author should not be made to wait for his money until the publisher has secured a large profit for himself.

In view of the facts that the assignment of the copyright is almost always demanded by the publisher, who in return almost always resents enquiry into his figures, it is asked—

*Is the method of " royalty," in any of its present forms,
a satisfactory one to writers ?"*

One cannot help thinking that it is most satisfactory to
those who know least about it.   In a recent magazine a
well-known writer contributed an article upon publishing,
in which the following words occur :—

" The terms on which the author lets out his manuscript,
in nine cases out of ten, are either that he shall receive a
royalty, or fixed payment, on all copies sold ; or half the
net profits of the venture—accounts being made up
periodically according to agreement.   If he have bargained
for a *royalty*, the author gets his payment on sales, whether
the book has yielded a profit to the capitalist or the
reverse.   If, on the other hand, he has bargained to receive
half-profits, the capitalist still takes all the risk.   The
worst that can happen to the author is that there is no
profit balance to divide.   The *royalty* system is so
obviously fair and reasonable that there is no need to say
much about it.   The *half-profits* system, however, I have
again and again heard loudly declaimed against in very
strong language."

It will be seen at once that this writer had no idea that
often the author contributes something towards bringing
out his work, that more often he receives no royalty till the
cost of production is covered ; that most often he receives
no royalty till a certain fixed number of copies have been
sold.   Again if a royalty of 30 per cent. is obviously fair,
what has he to say to a royalty of five per cent. ?

He is of course as much abroad in his allusions to the
half-profit system.

Theoretically, as has been freely allowed, the method
of paying an author in proportion to the sales of his work
is admirable.   When the practical working of the method
is looked at, it does not appear so admirable.

CHAPTER VI.

V.—PUBLISHING ON COMMISSION.

A VERY large and profitable branch of the publishing business is that known as Commission business, in which the author defrays the whole expense of production, and pays the publisher for his services as agent between him and the public.

Only those who have access to sources of information know how largely it is the custom to publish in this way. It is often the only method to be employed in dealing with philosophical, scientific, and technical works ; it is nearly always the only method of publishing poetry ; it is also responsible (as has before been said) for at least three-quarters of modern fiction.

If the agreement is fairly drawn and honestly carried out this method is just, and applicable to any form of literary property. Moreover, it has more than once been found, with slight modifications, to be the method by which the best pecuniary returns are secured to the author, at the price, however, of a great deal of trouble, which it would be impossible for any but a man of leisure to allow himself to incur. Reference especially is made to cases where the author has the work printed at his own expense, takes it to a publisher, and says, "Sell these books for so much each and account to me for so much on each copy ; keep the rest for your services." This entails upon the author a great deal of trouble, and presupposes in him considerable business knowledge, while none but a really good book would ever be issued by a publisher for him on such terms, unless the percentage surrendered were so high as practically to annul the benefits of the method.

Again, it is often advantageous to a man's reputation

that he should publish a book at his own expense, even though it may appear that he will never recover the money by its sale. Circumstances under which this is the case are quite easy to imagine.

These books should be published upon commission. All offers to share the risk will be accompanied by some condition which generally leads to the fleecing of the author under the name of "guarantee," "half-profit," or "half-risk." The expense to the author under these methods, although in each case the pecuniary risk purports to be divided between him and the publisher, has always, in the cases brought before the Society, proved actually larger than where the author has simply paid the whole cost. Invariably it will cost him more than if he had given his book upon commission to a good publisher.

Here is a proposal for publishing on commission :—

1. A fee of Two Guineas to be paid to Messrs. A. B. and Co. —hereinafter called the Publishers—previous to opening an account for the production and publication of a book.

2. The Publishers will supply Authors with estimates for the printing, &c., of works placed in their hands. They will charge a commission of 10 per cent. on the trade price for printing, paper, &c., and reserve to themselves the right to take the usual credit or the equivalent discount for cash payments. No cash discount shall exceed 7½ per cent.

3. A sufficient sum to meet the estimated charges for production and publication, including such a sum for advertising as the Author or Proprietor may deem desirable, to be paid to the Publishers before the work is sent to press.

4. The Publishers charge a commission of 10 per cent. on the sales.

5. All copies sold to be accounted for at the trade sales price, 25 as 24, or 13 as 12, less 5 per cent. to cover trade discounts.

6. If it be considered desirable to allow the trade any extra discounts beyond 5 per cent., which shall be left to the judgment and discretion of the Publishers, such discounts shall be debited in the account.

7. The Publishers' name only to be printed as Publishers on the title-page of the book, and it is to be sold only through their agency.

8. The entire management of the work shall be placed in the Publishers' hands.

Note in this agreement :—

(1.) The author is asked to assign the whole management of the book to the house. He ought to have a voice in the expenditure to be incurred over advertisement, and to have that expenditure regulated by a clause in the agreement.

(2.) The house takes a commission of 10 per cent. on the cost of production. This seems to hold out a direct inducement to make that cost high. No arrangement can be a good one where the principal and agent have opposing interests.

(3.) There is no clause giving the author the right to send an accountant to inspect the books, but it follows upon the latter objection that this is a precaution that should be taken.

Notwithstanding these objections, this is by far the most straightforward and satisfactory proposal for publishing upon this method that has come under the notice of the Society of Authors. The following rough calculation indicates the author's share of profits under it. The ordinary 6s. novel is used as an example.

It costs £75 to produce 1,000 copies, inclusive of moulding and stereotyping, but exclusive of advertisement. If the edition sold on the terms mentioned in clause 5 of the contract it would realise £175 at least.

The publishers would receive—

	£	s.	d.
Publishing fee	2	2	0
Commission on cost of production	7	10	0
„ sales	17	10	0
	£27	2	0

The author would receive £147 18s. He would have, however, to pay £75 for the production of the book, and—say £25 to £30 more for its advertisements. He would, at any rate, make over £40. If the book met with a large sale, as he need no longer incur so heavy an expense for advertisement as £25 on every 1,000 copies issued, and as the stereotyping has been paid for, the author's receipts would considerably increase. In fact, the figures show that publication under this proposal, in spite of its certain small faults, would give better results than under any proposal hitherto considered. The faults have been pointed out, to show the openings left for unscrupulous people.

The following is also a scheme for the production of a book upon the Commission method. It differs considerably in character from the preceding one.

FIRSTLY. The Publishers shall publish, advertise, and sell (and if so desired produce after the estimate hereunto attached) the work by the Author, and entitled "——————."

Should any legal proceedings, whether on account of Copyright, libel, or on any other account, having reference to or arising from the publication of this book, be instituted against the Publishers, the Author shall hold them good as regards any or all their expenses in connection therewith.

SECONDLY. The Publishers shall warehouse bound and quire stock, and deliver the usual press copies to the London journals, free of charge. On copies posted to the provincial and foreign press they shall charge only the forwarding costs.

THIRDLY. The Copyright and Plant of the work, and the rights of translation and reproduction, shall be the property of the Author, SUBJECT to his giving to the Publishers six calendar months' notice in writing of his intention to remove the publication from them.

FOURTHLY. The general management of the publication and sale (and if in their hands the production) of the work shall be left to the judgment and discretion of the Publishers.

FIFTHLY. The Publishers shall do their best to promote sales of the book, and in all ways treat it as though it were a publication in which their own sole interest were involved.

SIXTHLY. The Publishers shall account for all sales as thirteen as twelve at two-thirds of the selling price, less a discount of ten per centum thereupon, in consideration whereof (these being the Publishers' Trade "Journey Terms" upon which the greater portion only of their publications are sold) the Publishers shall make no charges for any sundry expenses of journeys, dinner, sales, commissions, bookings, telegrams, or postages that may be incurred in the interest of sales, PROVIDED ALWAYS, that should it be thought desirable to dispose of copies of the book, or of the "Remainder" or a part or parts thereof at a reduced price, or by auction, whether for the American, Colonial, Indian, or other foreign market or markets, or in England, then and in every such case the nett amount thus realised only shall be carried to the credit of the author.

SEVENTHLY. The Publishers shall charge a profit of ten per centum upon the nett amount of all sales as above, and a profit of five per centum upon all advertisements which shall be invoiced by them at the "scale" prices of the respective journals in which the advertisements appear.

EIGHTHLY. Accounts shall be made up every ―――― months

Estimate

For producing 1,000 copies of " ―――――," to form a volume of say 10 sheets of 16 pages in pica old style, 34 × 20.

	£	s.	d.
Composition, say 10 sheets, per sheet....	13	15	0
Stereotyping, say „	3	0	0
Corrections, say hours per hour of work			
Wood blocks and electros, blocks per block			
„ „ „ „			
„ „ „ „			
Coloured plates, plates, per plates			
Maps, maps per map....			
Binder's blocks....			
Paper, say 10 reams, double demy, per ream	12	10	0
Plate paper, reams „	1	5	0
Machining, say „ „	8	15	0
„ wood blocks	3	15	0
Binding, copies per copy	14	11	8
Preparation of MS. for press			
Publisher's reader			
Insurance (if required)	0	6	8
Sundry Incidental Expenses....			
Advertisements, say scale prices	5	0	0
	£62	18	4

Should the MS., with or without additions thereto in the proofs (if any), yield more or less than the estimated number of sheets, or should it be thought advisable to increase or reduce the expenditure by way of Advertisements, then and in every such case this Estimate will be affected *pro rata* in the items of Composition, Stereotyping, Paper, Machining and Binding, and Advertisements respectively.

It is difficult to believe that this is a proposal on the

part of the publishers to act as agents—pure and simple for the author, incurring no risk, and being paid beforehand for their trouble. It is impossible to believe that the publishers are treating the book " as though their own sole interests were involved."

First the book is to be produced " after the estimate attached." But this is largely in excess of the proper cost of production, as estimated by other and independent printers. As a matter of fact, the items " Composition," " Machining," " Paper," are double what they should be.

Here is the estimate of an independent printer for the same book :—

Demy 8vo., 122 pp. (including title and preface) 3 pp. plates, and doing up in lined coloured paper, printed cover, 1,000 copies, £28 nett.

Advertisements are, of course, not included.

There is no charge for correction or for stereotyping in this estimate of £28. These items would bring the cost of production to £40. The publishers' estimate contains no mention of stereotyping, but without it, amounts to £62 18s. 4d.

Again, the author has to pay ready money to the publisher. Will the publisher pay ready money to the printer? If he does, he will get discounts, but he nowhere offers to credit the author with them. If he does not, he secures interest on the author's money as long as he can obtain credit. Again why?

Note also that no arrangement is made about advertising. There is no suggestion that the author, who has to pay for them, will either be asked to what extent he wishes advertisements to appear, or will be permitted to satisfy himself, in the only way possible to him, that the book has received the advertisement paid for. The only suggestion under the head of advertising is that the publishers " should have five per cent. upon all advertisements invoiced by them at the 'scale' prices of the respective journals in which the advertisements appear." It is then to their direct interest to advertise as largely as they can. The author pays the money, and they take the percentage.

Next, the publishers receive ten per cent. on the result

of the sales, and ten per cent. on the nett profits. The former charge is clearly inadmissible if the latter is allowed.

Observe, lastly, the quaint air of proprietorship that the publishers assume in the author's private property. The author must give six months' notice in writing of his intention to remove the publication. He is to give them an equal interest with himself in foreign profits. They are to have the entire control of the production—advertisement arrangements included — yet they have a direct pecuniary interest in making the advertisement charges heavy.

It must be repeated that it is hard to believe that this is a proposal from the publishers to act as simple agents.

The agreement is a printed form!

Here is another agreement.

It purports to be a contract under which the author pays for the production of the book, and the publishers sell it, and give him the money, less ten per cent. for their services.

C. D., the Publishers, agree to publish the work entitled "————
————," for the said A. B., who on his part agrees to cede to them exclusively the right to publish the said work, on the conditions following ; the cost of production and all incidental expenses being at the exclusive risk of the said A. B. ; the publishing price being fixed at ————, the said C. D. account for the sales to the said A. B. at a deduction of one-third from the said publishing price, 13 copies as 12, being the average nett trade price, with the exception of any special sales at a reduced price that may be mutually agreed upon.

A commission of Ten per cent. to be charged by C. D. on the nett amount of all sales, they taking the risk of all debts.

Accounts to be made up half-annually, A. B. to be allowed one hundred copies without commission.

Under such a contract as this it is easy to see what might happen, if the publishers should choose to over-state the cost of production. The author has to pay for printing, paper, composition, &c., but his agreement does not contain a hint that he shall only pay the actual cost, and shall be allowed to satisfy himself that this is all that he has paid.

There is no arrangement of any kind about advertisement, and no limit set to the sum that might be spent in this way. The actual cost of the book may be run up to such a sum as to destroy all chance of any profit coming to the author, while the publisher, who has been at no risk, receives his percentage on all sales.

Lastly, the demand from an author of the copyright of a book, being published upon commission, is unique ; yet this is what is meant by the proposal that the author should cede to the publisher the exclusive right to publish his work.

There is another method of publishing, " The Guarantee Method," which may as well be discussed under " Commission " as anywhere else. It has already been alluded to. It is one that the publisher in this case especially recommends, saying that he often uses it, because it is " equitable." Yet the facts that he cannot lose by it, and may win by it, may also have influenced him in his preference, if only in a second degree to this singular passion for " equity."

"I have made," he writes to an author who had submitted a MS. to him, "a calculation, and I believe that your MS. will make a volume of some 160 pages crown octavo size ; if it is issued in this shape, well printed on good paper, and bound in extra cloth, gilt lettered, I shall be willing to publish the work on the following arrangement :—

" To take the entire responsibility of the production of the volume and all the expenses of publication and working on myself, if you will arrange to be responsible for the sale of 400 copies at 2s. 6d. each, or whatever number of copies are needed to bring the sales up to this quantity, if it has not been reached six months after the date of publication, the published price of the book being 4s. 6d.

" Thus, if we are unfortunate enough to sell only, say, 300 copies, I should ask you to take the remaining 100 at the price named ; if we reach the 400, you would not be troubled any further concerning payment. The plan is one that I have frequently worked upon, and is an *equitable* one, as the author is not responsible for the initial expense of production, advertising, reviewing, &c.,* and all sales during the six months go to the reduction of his liability, and if the work is fairly successful it is published without any expense to him whatever. Of course, if the work is a success and we get beyond the 400 copies, I shall be willing to pay a royalty of £2 5s. on each hundred copies sold after 450 copies have been disposed of by ordinary sales."

Such is the proposal.

The author, a person of some experience, wrote to ask, (1) for an estimate of the cost of production in detail, as he was to make himself liable for £50, and wished to know why £50 more than £5 or £105 ; (2) for a guarantee that his book would be advertised up to a certain figure, and only up to that figure—for it will be seen that under the original proposal all such details were left to the publisher.

The following was the publisher's reply :—

" The number of copies which we ask you to be responsible for of your proposed volume, is only just sufficient to secure us from loss in the venture should it not prove successful. We should print at least 750 copies of the work ; you would therefore be entitled to royalty on all copies sold, beginning with 451, up to the full 750 copies, after which, supposing we did not print more than the 750, we should, of course, have to make fresh arrangements for a second edition if called for.

" Of course, if the possibility of loss in the event of the book not selling would be inconvenient, I cannot recommend you to go on with it, as I should not like to be the means of leading you into a transaction which you would afterwards regret. We should advertise it in all the leading papers, both weekly and daily, and in such monthlies as may be deemed advisable according to the character of the book."

Neither of the author's questions is here answered. Surely, if the publisher's risk was really going to be £50, he should have no objection to proving it. Surely, if he

---

* Is it intended to hint that reviews have to be paid for, or is the publisher only magnifying the arduous task of sending out copies for review ?

intended to advertise the book, he should have no objection to saying to what extent.

Incidentally it is learned that the publisher intends to print 750 copies (" supposing he does not print more," whatever that may mean). Of these, one guesses 50 copies to be for the press. The first 400 copies are sold for the publisher's benefit at about 2s. 8d. each (which is the trade price of a 4s. 6d. book), exclusive of copies that may fetch more ; therefore the publisher intends to receive £53 6s. at least before the author receives anything. This is to reimburse him for expenses which he will not account for. 250 copies now have to be accounted for. At trade price these would fetch £33 6s. Of this the publisher, it seems, would be entitled to £28 3s. 6d., and the author to £5 2s. 6d. £5 2s. 6d. is the utmost the author *can* make under this agreement, and yet he stands to lose £50.

Lastly, as no details are vouchsafed, it is not known if the publisher intended to stereotype the work ; he can, if he likes, and it would seem that he can also produce and sell as many copies as he likes, always subject to the payment of the magnificent royalty of 10 per cent. on the full price. He need not do so unless he likes. If the book is a good one and meets with success, he can reap all the returns less a royalty of 10 per cent. ; if it is a bad one he need neither advertise nor stereotype—nor, indeed, do anything but print 400 copies, and receive from the author £50 for doing so, without proving that he has spent anything like that sum.

Let it not, however, be forgotten that the proposal found favour with him, because it was " equitable."

There is another variation of the commission method— it is publishing by subscription.

Here a certain number of people express themselves willing to take a copy or copies of the book at a certain price, and when enough subscriptions have been secured to obviate loss on the transaction, the author employs a publisher to issue the book.

It is a very old method, being, as is well known, the

plan upon which many of the poems and pamphlets of the seventeenth and eighteenth centuries were issued.

The remuneration which the publisher should receive depends upon the value of his services ; there is no risk. If the author brings all the subscribers, the publisher is only entitled to such a percentage on the sales as will repay him for his time and trouble. If the publisher have influence and use it on behalf of the book, he represents some of the capital collected to produce the book, and he should be proportionately rewarded.

County histories, and certain costly illustrated works, are very commonly issued in this way, and so far from there being any objection to the method, literature gains greatly by it, in that many books are published in this way which could never otherwise see the light. But without the precaution of an agreement, trouble may follow.

For instance an author published without agreement, upon the personal recommendation of a friend, with a firm of which he knew nothing whatever. The system of publishing suggested by that firm, on which one member of the firm says they may venture to issue the book, was that of " subscription."

The book appeared. There had been a large amount of " author's corrections," the responsibility for which was bandied from printer to author, and back again, as usual.

Then the author asked for accounts, and was told that they were no business of his, as profit or loss must be the publishers', whom alone the accounts concerned. They, in fact, appropriated his rights entirely, he having published with them without an agreement.

They resent the imputation of not being straightforward : cannot, they say, give accounts if they wished to, because they have not got the items, and lastly, while practically appropriating the book, they own that they have procured *no* subscribers, the only names having been brought by the author.

An agreement would have set all this right.

F

To sum up :—

To publish on commission is a good method, if the author is protected by a good agreement, as is shown by the results that would have obtained under the first agreement quoted in this chapter.

No agreement is a good one wherein :—

(1) The author does not absolutely retain his copyright.

(2) Wherein he can be cheated concerning the cost of production.*

(3) Wherein he has not entire control over the advertising for which he has to pay.

On the other hand, few authors have the knowledge, the time, and other qualities necessary to conduct their own publishing business.

In view of the facts (1) that the author is sometimes asked to assign his copyright, and (2) that he is almost invariably left at the publisher's mercy with regard to the cost of production and advertisement, the question is asked :—

Is publishing by commission, in any of its forms, entirely satisfactory to writers ?

---

* A publisher, of course, has a right to say " I will produce your book for £80 giving no details." This does not mean, he says, that it will cost him £80 to produce it, but that he estimates his services under the head of production at that sum. But a publisher has no right to say " I will produce your book for £80, because that is what it will actually cost me," and to render accounts to show that he has spent £80, when in reality (as his printer's bills would show) he has spent nothing of the sort. This is a fraud.

CHAPTER VII.

ADVERTISEMENT.

ALL books must have advertisement, and from a very ancient date this necessity has been recognised by those interested in their sale. "If the book please you," writes Cicero to Atticus, "you will take care to have it circulated in Athens, and other cities of Greece." Absolutely the first "posters" ever seen in England were those by which Caxton advertised certain devotional tablets of his own printing, while the first regular newspaper advertisers were the booksellers.

It is on their presumed experience in advertising that publishers have chiefly grounded the necessity for their own existence; yet, curiously enough, there is no item in a publisher's account more bewildering to the author. He soon perceives that the size of the original edition, the original cost of the production of the book, and the number of sales effected, have no fixed relation to the amount spent in this manner; and he wonders upon what system, if any, the money has been expended. Disputes on the subject are therefore frequent, as might be expected from the almost invariable manner of presenting the account. This is to charge a lump sum, giving neither details nor vouchers in proof of the same. Such a way of doing things makes it so incredibly easy for a publisher to cheat, that to the man of business, accustomed always to know for what he is paying, it becomes incredibly hard to believe that he has not been cheated.

It is proposed to consider the advertisement of a book, and to call attention to the boundless faith that nearly every publisher requires of his clients, and to mention a few of the obvious ways in which an author, falling into the hands of the unscrupulous, might be cheated.

The subject will be treated very briefly.

It forms a great part of a publisher's skill, the part on which he most insists, to find out how much should be spent on advertising a book, and where the money should be laid out. For in respect to advertising publishing is not like other trades. It seems impossible for other tradesmen to spend too much in bringing their wares before the public, but there is a limit to the amount which should be spent upon a book, and this it is the part of the wise publisher to determine. Experience should enable him to ascertain what each book will "bear," for, as has been remarked, a book cannot be crammed down the public throat like soothing syrup.

The possible field for a book is not unlimited ; it is no use advertising them when the libraries and the trade have taken all they are likely to want ; if a book is going to go at all, it will, after a time, advertise itself. Some books, again, it is found by experience, want very little advertising, while others do not go off without a great deal. On one of the most successful of recent books it was found necessary to spend over £80 in advertisements before it really began to move. Once started it went off rapidly, and in a few weeks there were sold 10,000 copies and more. Roughly speaking, if a book gets no indirect advertisement, either through being on a subject which is attracting public interest, or through being the production of a well-known man, it may be necessary, if it is likely to reach in the end a large sale, to give it a great deal of direct advertisement in the papers. Where a great amount of indirect advertisement is sure to be given to a book, it seems to be waste of money to spend much upon newspaper insertions.

Some daily papers are better for book advertisements than others, and some weekly papers are better than others. It is cheaper to advertise in some papers than others. The subject of some books may make it advisable to have them mentioned in special papers, which are useless for ordinary advertisement.

There is undoubtedly much to think about, and if the publisher could give assistance that could be relied upon in all these matters his services would be most valuable. But his knowledge is apt to be capricious. As regards his own book he may know ; as regards an author's book he seems not to be so certain. In cases where the cost of advertisement, among other items of production, is left in the publisher's hands, with the understanding that the author will pay, he seems, if we may judge by results, neither to know how much to spend, nor in what direction to spend it. But if it be assumed, and it has been very vehemently claimed for him, that the wise publisher is an expert in the science and art of advertisement, what adjective are we to apply to the publisher whose unsaleable books are always burdened by costly advertisement, of which he is only prepared to render the account as a lump sum?

In one account the charge was verified. The book had really been made to carry the enormous sum of £222 2s. 2d. for advertisement, but this abuse of the discretion left in the publisher's hands ruined the financial position of the work.

The following can only be considered as samples, so numerous are the methods by which wholesale cheating is carried on by the unscrupulous under the name of advertisement. Most of them, it will be at once perceived, are only possible because the accounts are not properly rendered, it being considered sufficient to tell an author that he is £60 or £160 in debt, without giving further detail. Where there is no check it is only a question which of many tricks to choose. Instances of sharp practice or fraud by each method alluded to are well known to the Society of Authors to have occurred.

1. A lump sum is added to the money actually spent in advertising.

2. A percentage is added to the money actually spent.

3. All the money that has been spent by the firm in a given period in advertising is divided among all the books alike, although an "author's book" may have figured very seldom in comparison with those in whose sale the publisher is more directly interested.

4. An arrangement is made with a paper by which a certain nominal sum is charged and a large discount allowed. The author is charged the nominal price. This allowance is never granted by any of the great papers, but constantly by the young and struggling journals. An instance is known of a certain weekly paper which at one period of its existence allowed a publisher 90 per cent. discount on the nominal price!

5. A publisher sometimes engages a space in a journal every day or every week for a certain period. If he has no books of his own with which he can profitably fill it he takes an "author's book," fills this space with it, and charges the book with the whole cost for the week. Then he calls upon the author to admire his sagacity and enterprise in giving his book a "displayed advertisement," concealing the fact that the book is not one that could bear this expense, or be any the better for it. This, however, is very often the explanation of displayed advertisements of books, which do not seem worth this lavish expenditure. It is a practice which appears advantageous to the author, who is naturally pleased to see his book thus freely advertised. When, however, he finds what he has to pay for such display he is sometimes not so pleased.

6. A charge is made for advertisement of the book in the publisher's own magazines. With this actual fact we are not quarrelling ; the publisher has certainly a right to charge for the advertisement of a book in his own magazine. But if advertisement is to be paid for by the author, or if the book is published on a half-profit system, or any system where the author is interested in the amount

spent on publishing, he ought to be asked beforehand if he consents to advertise in his publisher's magazine at all, and, if so, to what extent ; otherwise the publisher makes by this process a separate profit. Moreover, the process can be made a very profitable one to the publishers. There was, for example, a certain firm which issued a periodical, of which all that need be said is that its circulation was assuredly small. This firm in rendering accounts invariably charged a lump sum for advertising, and on being questioned indignantly refered the author to a mention of the title of his book in the list of publications at the end of this magazine. It is evident that insertion in a list at the end of a worthless periodical is not a short cut to publicity for a book.

Another point may also arise. Is it a straightforward action for a publisher to charge an author for advertisement where by an arrangement of exchange he has himself nothing to pay ? That is to say, A and B, two publishers, who both have magazines, may exchange pages of advertisement. The author, we will suppose—the case is so common—is liable for the expense of advertisement over which the publisher A has complete control. By this arrangement with the publisher B, A gets the advertisement for nothing and charges the author for it. He thus makes a secret and underhand profit. In addition, whatever the circulation of B's magazine may be, A will have a bias towards advertising his authors' books in it.

Again, A may send a sheet of advertisement to B and *pay for it*, subsequently, without anything more than tacit understanding, B sends A a sheet and pays for it. Manifestly, having paid the money, it is right and proper to charge it against the book. The author is not injured unless, *which there is nothing to prevent*, the advertisement is inserted oftener and at greater expense than the book will bear. But this is the very thing which may too often indirectly or directly benefit his publisher.

7. A charge is made for inserting the book in the publisher's own lists. Most publishers have such lists,

which they put into their own books, and otherwise give and send about among the trades.

It is to the publisher's interest to send this list about, and to have it as large as possible, and as complete as possible ; it is therefore ridiculous that the author should ever be called upon to share the expense. He might just as logically be invited to contribute towards painting the publisher's name over his office door.

Most of these tricks can be prevented very simply. First, the author must insist upon having a detailed account given him of the advertisements with which he is charged. Second, he must be informed beforehand in what channels the publisher means to advertise, so that he may have a chance of objecting, if he thinks that the publisher has any reason for choosing those channels other than the welfare of the book. He must, in short, have a voice in the management of the advertisements, if he has got to pay for them. The author is probably ignorant of many of these things, and would not know how to exercise his power when he obtained it, but it would be easy for him to seek counsel of those whose business it is to know.

The best advertisement that a book can have is to be talked about by its readers ; good reviews are also most valuable ; and even notices which are not all laudatory, have a value from their number. These indirect advertisements help a book immensely. In a case where they may be expected, it is clearly bad management to spend a lot of money in direct advertising until the extent and result of such gratuitous advertisement is known. More, it is foolish to go on spending money in direct advertisement when it is certain that no one will recommend the book to his neighbour. What direct advertisement does is to prevent the book from being still-born. By securing some little attention for it, it becomes probable that any merits the book may have will be discovered. "My own opinion," an author of experience writes, " is that most books require very little advertising. The subject attracts a certain number, the style others. If it be a story and a good one, the good news that there is actually another clever novel in the field, generally runs like wildfire. If it be a dull story, no amount of advertising will do it any good." We agree with this author. Much of the money spent in advertising is absolutely thrown away ; and I believe that even honest publishers who do not play tricks with their advertisements put too much confidence in them. A "shilling dreadful" some two years ago achieved a tremendous success after tremendous advertisement, and this book is often alluded to as a triumph of successful advertising. It was nothing of the sort. The very wide and clever advertisement brought the book within the ken of a very uncritical public, wanting, and ever wanting, an exciting story. Those who read it found that it *was* exciting, and told their neighbours. It is true that from a literary point of view the book was a very poor one, but, at any rate to a very large class, it was exciting, therefore, and not directly because of the copious advertising, it succeeded.

Direct advertisement is only an important affair to those who are themselves incurring the expenses of producing their works. The advertising of the work which is produced at the publisher's expense may be left to their experience. In the former case it is absolutely necessary that the author should have a clause in his agreement stipulating that he will only, at first, be liable for advertisement up to a certain figure, and shall be at liberty to demand proof that his book *has* been advertised up to that figure. He must also have a voice in the choice of the papers, and if he feels that he has obtained a discretion he cannot make use of, he should take advice from those able to give it.

From every single agreement in the possession of the Society these stipulations are absent.

Of all the complaints received by us, the commonest is that the publisher has charged for advertisements, which have never been inserted. As this has undoubtedly been done, generally in one of the ways indicated above, it would most certainly be in the true interests of both author and publisher that the chance of such dishonesty should for the future be obviated by the invariable insertion of some such stipulations.

The remarks that have gone before are pertinent only to those cases where the author *knows* that he has to pay the advertisement charges, but is not provided with an agreement by which he can regulate the charges. There is another wholesale way of cheating the author, and that is to make him liable for advertisement charges which he, in his ignorance, believes will be defrayed by the publisher. This is generally done in the following way :—An estimate is given to the author for the cost of production of his book—without details—and he finds, after having incurred the expense of printing, &c., that, unless he spends more money to have the book advertised it cannot be said to be published at all. The cost of advertisement is not included in the estimate. A proper clause in the agreement on the subject would of course put a stop to such proceedings, as much as to any of the tricks already mentioned. Let the author mistrust the proposal in which advertisement is not mentioned at all, even more than he does the one where it is mentioned, only to be left in the publisher's hands.

CHAPTER VIII.

AUTHOR'S CORRECTIONS.

IN the introduction to " The Cost of Production," a
pamphlet privately issued to our members, allusion has been
made to this subject in the following words : " Here, as in
other details of the publishing trade, no method prevails ; no
settled charges allow the author to estimate how much he
may correct, and how he may escape an enormous addition
to the Cost of Production."

In proof of this it is only necessary to refer back to the
publishing transactions detailed in Chapters IV. and V.

The offer made in the agreement* which accompanied
the estimate given on page 39 ran as follows :—

" The expenses, of the author's proof corrections to the
extent of one-half pound sterling, as per schedule, shall be
debited to the first account, but should such expenses
exceed this amount the author shall refund the excess to
the publisher on publication of the work." The estimate,
is for the half-profit production of a book of nine
sheets of sixteen pages a sheet. Therefore, of the ten
shillings only five comes out of the publisher's pocket, and
this is the extent to which they will be liable for expenses
incurred in " author's corrections." A fraction over sixpence per sheet ! In this agreement then the expenses of
author's corrections cannot be estimated from the same
standpoint as in most of those which follow, where something between five and ten shillings per sheet is always
provided for. But by looking at the estimate we find
that a reason is given for the charge. Ten shillings is

---

* The agreement itself was very similar in terms to the second one
in the same chapter.

charged because it is probable that ten hours of a printer's time, at one shilling per hour, will be required to effect the corrections. This is tangible. May it then be assumed in the case, shortly to follow, where £106 13*s.* was charged for "corrections and cancelled matter," that it took a man nine months at eight hours a day, exclusive of Sundays, to effect the corrections? Again, if the publisher liked later to say that there was £100 more owing to him for corrections, one of his men having been assiduously engaged for a year in making them, the author would under this agreement have to pay, or go to law to dispute the charge.

Under the next agreement in this chapter the publisher offers to undertake the cost of "corrections and altera- tions" up to ten shillings for every sixteen pages of print.

Under the next agreement the publisher offers to debit the account for which he and the author are jointly liable with £10 for "corrections." That is, the publisher under- takes the cost of "author's corrections" up to £5. The book is one of 46 sheets (*vide* estimate), so that the author is really allowed to correct gratis to the extent of 2*s.* 3*d.* per sheet (about). This offer is not munificent, *but* it comes from the same firm who in an exactly analogous case offered to allow the author to correct up to not quite sixpence half- penny per sheet gratis. From what standpoint can this firm be working? Again, as under their other contract, the publisher is at liberty to charge for "author's correc- tions" what he likes, and can recover anything in excess of £10 from the author.

The "half-profit dodger" does not mention "author's corrections" in his letter of agreement. His bill for them is the first allusion to the subject that he makes.

Now turn to Chapter V.

Under the first agreement the publisher offers to under- take the cost of "author's corrections" to the extent of £6. In the second transaction the charge for "author's corrections and cancelled matter" is £106 13*s.*, being a much larger sum than was charged for the original setting of the type. A liberal reduction was accepted.

In the third transaction the publisher offers to undertake the cost of " author's corrections" to the extent of £3.

In the fourth the subject of " author's corrections" is not alluded to. Note, however, that by the fourth clause of this agreement the author is held liable " for any loss there may be on account of the publication of the book." What, save honesty, is to prevent the publisher from stating the cost of " author's corrections" to have been (say) £100. It is better for the author that the matter should be mentioned, even if he cannot understand the terms in which it is mentioned.

In the next agreement the publisher undertakes the cost of "corrections other than printer's errors," up to an average sum of ten shillings per sheet of sixteen pages.

Generally, then, it appears that the agreement provides that "author's corrections beyond ten shillings a sheet will be charged for." Some agreements substitute for ten shillings, five shillings, or fifteen shillings, or twelve shillings. Some we have seen come down to sixpence halfpenny. Some allude to a sheet of sixteen pages, some to a sheet of thirty-two pages. Some charge a lump sum for the whole book, without alluding to pages. There is evidently no uniform charge, each proposal being dictated by the publisher's caprice. But, taking as an example the proposal that all corrections beyond ten shillings a sheet will be charged for, what does the proposal mean? Clearly that in every sixteen pages the author shall be allowed to make corrections to the extent indicated by the payment of ten shillings to the compositor who has to make the alterations. To what extent is this? What author knows? For that matter who knows?

It is obvious that if an author practically re-writes his work he must pay for re-composition, but every agreement should be so worded that :—

Firstly, and chiefly, by being alluded to, this charge cannot be sprung suddenly upon the author as an extra expense.

Secondly, the author shall not have to pay for the errors of the publisher's workmen.

And thirdly, if the author is charged under this head, and is allowed fifteen shillings a sheet gratis, (or for that matter sixpence halfpenny), he shall be allowed to see the charge for corrections in the printer's bill, and satisfy himself that his publisher has really incurred the extra expense he alleges in his account, and incurred them for proof-corrections only.

A bill for £114 5s. was presented to certain members of the Society as the cost of author's corrections made in a musical score. The book was one of thirty sheets, and £22 10s. was deducted from this sum according to an agreement, allowing corrections gratis up to fifteen shillings a sheet.

The musical editor declared that he could have incurred no such enormous charge. Accounts were applied for, but at first in vain.

At last—seven months after the rendering of the first account—a bill with details was given them. And here it is :—

	£	s.	d.
Alterations and corrections, also resetting matter throughout entire work, 900 hours at 1s. 6d. (reader's time in revising included)	67	10	0
Time in pulling extra proofs and revises, paper, &c.	27	0	0
Postage of ditto £4 10 0			
An allowance of 1 10 0			
	3	0	0
To Plate proof of entire work	13	0	0
Plate corrections in ditto and type	3	15	0
	£114	5	0

£67 10s. the authors did not dispute, though they did not believe they had properly incurred such a charge. It is quite easy, however, to see that to correct music may be a costly and difficult task.

For the rest they very properly denied their liability.

The cost of the postage of proofs and of the paper they are printed upon, cannot be legitimately included under the head of "author's corrections."

As has already been said, the subject is one which is constantly giving rise to dispute, and which therefore calls loudly for some improved method of treatment.

CHAPTER IX.

AGREEMENTS, MORE OR LESS.

THE details of the more ordinary forms of the contracts under which authors dispose of their property have now been discussed. But there are two ways in which the author, independently of detail, can go wholly wrong from the outset. One may be called the way of too much agreement—the other that of no agreement at all.

We will consider the latter first.

In every business transaction, save one between man and man, the experience of ages has caused it to be assumed, without offence being thereby given or thereat taken, that an agreement must be drawn up so as to give neither party any opportunity to overreach the other. When a man has a property to dispose of and when another is ready to purchase the same, each goes, as a matter of course, to a solicitor, or other independent adviser, and obtains, often at considerable cost, all the protection against overreaching that can be derived from skilled counsel.

This protection takes the form of a document, wherein is embodied, over mutual signature, the terms of the proposed transfer. To the clauses of this document each of the contracting parties can be bound tightly down, neither therefore signs it without due consideration and expert advice.

Even the possessor of a five-shilling share in a Capel Court bubble has some documentary protection, for promoters are, at any rate in modern times, required to justify their prospectus more or less by their works.

In publishing transactions alone, where the interests represented may amount to many thousands, and the returns from a single book may be a substantial income, there are often no agreements.

Yet consider the attitude towards his work of the author who publishes without the protection of any written agreement whatever. Imagine a man to have built a house, and to go to a total stranger and say to him, " Take my house for forty years or more, do what you like with it, and give me in return whatever you think fit, say five-hundred pounds a year, or˙two dollars a week. I shall be satisfied with the reputation of having built such a very fine place." This man's ambitious soul would not save him from a vulgar fate, for his neighbours would think him an ass, and if the house should become valuable property, as might happen later, his relations would probably put him in an asylum, lest he should dispose of any more houses in a similarly artistic spirit.

There is no reason why the man who publishes without the protection of an agreement should be treated in any other way.

Here is a case.

A short time ago a book was brought out by a well-known publisher which, for one reason or another, achieved a large sale, and ran into three editions—three genuine different editions. The author got very little money indeed out of the book, only some twenty or thirty pounds. This was due to the easy-going way in which the arrangements for publication had been made. No formality, no annoying business routine. The publisher, in a note to a third person, one of his clients, about a totally different matter, said that he would consider the publication of this novel, (which had been mentioned to him by the third person,) on the half-profit system. No agreement was entered into by the author, but the MS. was sent to the publisher on those terms !

He published the book, and interpreted the terms as follows :—

G

(1) Assignment of the copyright to himself for ever, so that he could issue as many editions as he liked.

(2) Acceptation of his figures, and that without dispute, so that if ever the author's share looked like getting a big one, he could increase the expense of publication (on paper), and keep him within bounds.

(3) A final division of profit—according to his own figures, in the proportion of one-third to two-thirds.

This author had no remedy. By giving the publisher the unlimited right to produce, he practically gave him the copyright, and exacted from him in return nothing whatever.

He almost got what he exacted.

Almost worse for the author than to have no agreement at all is to have an agreement dealing with future works, as well as with present ones.

It frequently happens that a publisher, in making terms with an author for one book pins him down in the agreement to write another book for him, to be issued on the same terms. This may be logical on the part of the publisher, or it may be crafty, but it is always apt to lead to dissension.

The publisher's idea is, that if an author can be tied down to write for him two or three consecutive books, and a profit can be made upon any one of them, this profit can be kept back to pay for losses over the others. If, on the other hand, they all prove successful, the publisher gets the two later books upon terms which he could not have hoped to get them, if the author had gone to him after a first success.

Several of these cases have come before the Society of Authors. Here is an agreement based upon this principle.

1. The Publisher engages to be at the sole expense of printing, binding, and advertising the work in question, and to pay to the Author one-half of all profits that may be derived from its sale after the cost of producing and advertising the said work has been defrayed. The remaining half profits are to belong to the Publisher in consideration

of the risk incurred by him in producing and advertising the said work and of his publishing it without charging the customary publishing commission.

2. The size and form of the said work and the price at which it shall be published is left to the discretion of the Publisher.

3. The Publisher engages to render to the Author the half-yearly accounts of the sales of the work in question on the usual trade terms, less any discounts and commissions allowed by him, and to pay to the Author the half profits that may be due to him in cash.

4. The Publisher further engages that after rendering the accounts as aforesaid, the books of the Publisher shall be open to the inspection of the said Author or his representative, so far as particulars of sales of the work in question are concerned.

5. The Author engages on his part that the publication and sale of the said work shall be exclusively in the hands of the Publisher.

6. The Author also engages that the next novel written by him shall be published by the Publisher on the same terms as "————" and further that his third novel shall also be published by him on the terms of paying him three-fifths of the profits arising from its sale after the cost of production and advertising has been defrayed, the remaining profits in either instance to belong to the Publisher in consideration of the risk incurred by him and of his publishing the works in question without charging the usual publisher's commission.

7. That the Author is to have the option of receiving payments in cash from the Publisher for the Copyright of the said third novel, or for a certain number of editions of it, in lieu of three-fifths of the profits arising from its sale, the said payment to be calculated on the basis of the profits that have been realised from the sales of the first two novels of the Author referred to in this agreement.

8. Should any dispute arise under this agreement, both parties hereby bind themselves to refer the same to arbitration in the usual way.

With regard to this agreement it should be re-marked :—

What is the customary publishing commission ?

Surely the ceding of half profits to the publisher is sufficient payment to him. He certainly would not undertake to publish at his own risk if he did not believe that there were going to be profits to share. This is the kind of suggestion too common in such contracts. It is intended to make the author believe that, in his favour. some undeniable rights of the publisher are being waived. There is no customary publishing commission in half-profit transactions.

In clause (4) there is a distinct advance. The very thing described by some publishers as preposterous, the demand for which has, in times gone-by but recent, been stigmatised by others as insolent—the opening of the publisher's books to the author's inspection—is here offered. But it is offered with a limit. The author is to be allowed to verify his doubts as to the particulars of sales. But this is a half-profit agreement. The particulars with which the author is most concerned, are those of the cost of production and advertisement, for till those be covered he does not begin to get any money. Again the next clause (5) expressly stipulates that the publication shall be left exclusively in the publisher's hands. This means that the publisher shall spend as much as he likes upon publishing and advertisement, shall not have to account for it in detail, and shall not have to pay the author anything until this unvouched expenditure is covered.

In clause (6) is the proposal to which exception is taken. Why should the author bind himself down to two more undertakings, one at the original terms, and the other at terms not much more advantageous?

Still more, why should he do it before he sees how the first book goes, and how far he wishes to continue to employ the publisher?

Lastly, the author has the option of taking a sum down for the copyright of his third book. This is to be calculated on the basis of the profits realised by the sales of the first two books. But how is the author to know what their profits really are? Only by having placed before him the actual sums incurred by the publisher in producing and advertising the book, and certainly not by taking for granted that the publisher's figures are the printer's facts.

One enterprising publisher proposed that the author of a fairly successful book should write for him exclusively for five years! When the proposition was made the author's book was in the seventh edition (or was stated to be so on the cover), but the receipts had not yet covered the cost of its production (or were stated not to have done so). It is a most amazing thing, but this author employed a solicitor to act between himself and the publisher, and the solicitor thought that the suggestion was a *fair* one! He had not grasped in the least that a selling book was a valuable property, and was quite willing to hand over all his client's possible rights for five long years upon terms which, by the case already before him, were evidently most unsatisfactory to the author.

Agreements binding down the author to write future work for the publisher are to be strictly avoided.

CHAPTER X.

REMAINDER-SALES.

THERE is constant difficulty upon this point. A large edition of a book gets left upon the publisher's hands under all sorts of circumstances, and his right to dispose of it depends upon those circumstances.

He may have originally produced too large an edition, for a publisher cannot make the public buy a book they do not want, and no one can always guess what book the public will want. He may have never made any attempt to get rid, in the usual manner, of what he has produced. For instance, on page 35, we have given an example of an agreement where it would be directly to the publisher's advantage not to get rid of more than a certain number of copies. Again, in cases where a large royalty is to be paid upon sales, only after a certain number of sales have been effected, or, under the " guarantee system," when a royalty is to be paid only after the guaranteed number have been sold, it is easy to understand (though the fact may be hard to believe) that occasionally it becomes to the publisher's pecuniary interest not to sell a book. Lastly, a publisher may not be able to get rid of what he has printed, irrespective of the matter of the book, because he himself is not recognised by the big booksellers as a person from whom a saleable book is ever got.

But whatever may be the circumstances, the publisher often has left in his possession a large stock. No one expects him to warehouse a book, no longer in demand at his own expense, even though it may be his fault that the book has not sold better. But what ought he to do, and what does he do?

In the case of the person last alluded to, his reason for

selling the remainder stock is want of ready money. There
is in 'London, at the present moment, an individual
masquerading as a publisher, who does not send round
the few books he ever produces to the trade at all. They
remain in his offices when they arrive from the printer, and
they are sold for 2d. each when he has to meet a bill. All
these books have been paid for by their authors. It is only
possible to warn young authors that these things happen,
that these people exist, and that if they will not ask advice
from those who know, before signing agreements with, and
giving cheques to, firms with grandiloquent titles and no
status, this is the kind of treatment they may meet with.

But apart from such impudent rogues (for whose
methods it would seem legal correction is difficult to
obtain), the ordinary publisher deals with his remainder
stock in a way that leaves much to desire.

His almost invariable practice is, having decided that
no further good can come to him from its retention, to
sell the book off for what he can get, without consulting
the author, without advising the author of his intention,
and as often as not without giving the author a share of
the result.*

Now this is an unwarrantable proceeding in every case,
except the rare one where the book has become by
purchase the sole and unquestioned property of the publisher. Then, of course, he can do what he likes with *his*
property. The author who has any pecuniary interest in
the sale of his book ought to have warning when his
book is about to be sold in this way, and should insist in
the agreement that he should have such warning. Moreover, he ought to have the chance of buying the edition at
such a sale price as is generally realised—say 2d. a volume
—subject to the publisher's proportionate lien upon the
book, and he ought to have a voice in deciding when
sales have ceased. It has before now happened that a

---

* *Vide* all the agreements.in Chapters IV. and V. The publisher,
it will be seen, can sell the stock as remainders entirely at his own
discretion.

book has been sold as a "remainder," and afterwards been in considerable demand. It is not far-fetched to imagine an ingenious and unscrupulous publisher actually buying the remainder stock himself at a ridiculously low price, and rendering to the author the guaranteed share of the results. Then the book is his own, the author having been paid off. The results of later sales will come to the publisher alone, undivided, and unquestioned.

The following is a case of constant occurrence.

An author has a pecuniary interest, as well as a personal interest, in the sale of a book for which his publisher assures him there is no longer any demand. As often as not the publisher has refused (which, of course, he has a perfect right to do) to advertise the book any further. Another publisher offers to publish the book. The author cannot get it into his possession without buying the remainder stock at trade price, and cannot republish without doing so, because his original publisher could always undersell his new publisher. Yet he knows that all that his original publisher will ever do with the book is to sell it as waste paper. To make the position still more galling, very often the author has paid—and overpaid —for the production of the work.

It is clear that this is a position against which the author must protect himself by a clause in his agreement.

There are many cases in the archives of the Society of Authors to prove that the question of remainder-sales is one that wants especial attention.

Here is such a case.

An author produced a book with a well-known firm of publishers on the half-profit system. They estimated the cost of producing the book at £109 12s. for 5,000 copies. The author thought a *smaller* edition would be sufficient, so they sent him an estimate for that, and it turned out to be £112 16s. 4d. for 1,000 copies! He paid the firm half this sum : and by the estimate of an independent printer he then paid them £20 more than the edition cost. By this time he had recognised, what a person of experience would have started by knowing, that the sale of a 1s. book is nothing, till it runs into tens of thousands. The chance, however, of his book ever doing this was rather small, for without giving him any notice, it was sold by the publishers as a remainder within a year of its publication.

No method of publishing, under which an author can be treated in such a manner, can ever be satisfactory to him. Yet this is the treatment he but too often receives.

CHAPTER XI.

CONCLUDING REMARKS.

SUCH are the usual methods of publishing. Such are the practices prevalent therein. Such is, and has been for years, the way in which a property is disposed of, which brings to its possessors an aggregate income of millions annually.

What fraction of this income in the aggregate reaches the creators it is impossible to guess, but, after allowing for the fact that certain authors are in a position to make comparatively good terms for themselves, it can be confidently stated that the fraction is a small one.

The best terms exacted for himself by the most popular novelist of the day are only good because they are better than those obtained by anyone else : they do not represent his due share of the profits of the work he has created.

I do not think that the manner in which the methods of publishing have been here considered can be called by anyone other than fair. Actual documents upon which publishing transactions have been entered into have been used, and actual figures arising out of those documents.

The following are the broad conclusions that it is thought may be drawn from them.

(1) The method of outright sale is open to but one objection, but that is a radical one.

The prices offered are inadequate.

(2) Any method of limited sale is better, but it is not often that the author gets an opportunity of issuing his works in this manner.

The most usual suggestion under this method is, that for a certain sum, he should cede his copyright until a certain number of copies have been sold. The fatal objection to this is, that no opportunity is given to him of proving that no more than the stipulated number have been sold. His suggestion that a clause providing him with this opportunity should be put into the agreement would formerly have been treated by the publisher as an insult, and would not, I think, be approved of now.

(3) The half-profit system is open to objections every whit as fatal.

There are almost never any profits to halve.

When there are profits they are almost never divided into halves.

As the author never knows how much the real initial expenditure has been, he can never know what the profits are, and hence what his half share should be.

If an author did actually receive the real half of the profits accruing from the sale of his work, we make bold to say that even then he is badly treated. A larger share than half is due to the brain that created the work.

(4) The royalty system in all its forms is open to some objections.

The royalty offered is generally a miserable one.

There is generally an attempt (equally generally a successful attempt) made by the publisher to secure the copyright of the book, so that for ever the author's remuneration must remain a miserable one.

If the royalty is to be paid only after a certain number of copies have been sold, the author never has an opportunity of finding out when the sales have reached that number. As, moreover, he is always required to leave all the management of the publication in his agent's hands, the agent has only to leave off acting, and the sales will never reach the number.

Where the royalty is to be paid only after the cost of production has been covered, the author never has an opportunity of finding out either what the real cost of production has been, or when the sales have been sufficient to effect this happy result. Moreover, as he is always required to leave all the management of the publication in his agent's hands, the agent has only to swell the cost of production, and the sales will NEVER realise the necessary sum. As an extra inducement to the agent to behave in this manner, we see that he very frequently by the express terms of the agreement receives 10 per cent. on the alleged cost.

Publishing on commission is only preferable to these methods. It is open to many objections.

Capital is required.

Rubbish finds its way into the market under this method, to the exasperation of the public, and, to a certain extent, to the detriment of work that is not rubbish. The same objection must be taken to those forms of royalty or half-profit publishing where the initial expense is defrayed by the author.

Secret profits are often, and can always, under prevailing methods be made by the publisher on the cost of production and advertisement of the book. Then, satisfied with having made a profit somehow to start with, he is apt to neglect the future of the book.

The fees demanded in return for services rendered are sometimes excessive.

Under every method the author is placed in an unfair position—that is, a position where he can be cheated with impunity — especially with regard to advertisements, "author's corrections," and sale of "remainder stock."

In every manner the author is made to feel that his rights of property are theoretical, and that his claim to the pecuniary return of his work is a monstrous exaction, to be resisted in every direction.

The way in which accounts are too often rendered to an author would not be tolerated in other business transactions. It is generally stipulated in the agreement that accounts should be made up every six months. Time after time authors complain that they cannot get this done. The publisher says that the sales are so small that it is not worth while to account for them, which is about as sensible as if a man were to say that he would not pay the income tax, because it was such a little one.

Now what happens? The author, ashamed of having produced a book that appears not to be wanted by the public, and to be a nuisance to his publisher, takes it for granted that his work is a failure, and after the first statement of accounts is content to hear no more about his work. After a time the publisher sells off the remainder, in the way that has been mentioned, without telling the author anything about it, and consequently without giving him his miserable share of such a sale.

How is the author to know how the book is progressing if he cannot get accounts rendered? Why should he take the publisher's word that there have been no sales worth mentioning? It is bad enough that the author should have accounts rendered to him in a way that he cannot understand, whose details are all unverified, but even that is better than having no account at all.

It is worth mentioning that after an author's death accounts frequently cease to be rendered. That appears to be the effect that death has upon a publishing transaction.

A grievance, occasionally, is the detention of MSS. Here the author is certainly often unreasonable. Vast quantities of hopeless rubbish are poured into the offices of a London publisher, and the author ought not to expect that a decision can be given upon his work within a few hours of its reaching the publisher's hands. So many people take up the trade of literature, without having one single quality to fit them for it, that a well-known publisher of fiction is often in receipt of over a dozen MSS. per diem. Such a firm may be excused if they are not in a position to give an opinion upon a work for a considerable period. But unfortunately the half-profit dodger is prompt. He can afford to be, because, as he never takes any risk and always makes considerable secret profits, he need not go through the form of reading a MS. before returning to the author an eulogistic opinion on its merits, together with an offer to produce it on receipt of a cheque. Alas! those who do not know him are apt to look upon this promptitude as courtesy.

Still, sometimes a MS. is kept an unconscionable time and there is difficulty in its recovery. A lady sent, in response to an advertisement, a manuscript to a small ready-money bookseller. The man was prepared to issue books at the author's expense, which doubtless seemed to him to justify his claim to advertise as a Publishing Company. Apparently she did not give him as much money as he wanted, for he would not produce the book, and she could not recover the manuscript. The "publisher" was called upon by a representative of the Society of Authors, when he said, with oaths :—

That he had not had the MS.

That he had sent it back.

That he would not send it back until the carriage was paid.

That he would burn it, a thing he had often done before with MSS. !

On being advised to be careful he sent the MS. back.

There is only one moral to be drawn from this story. Where an author is entirely ignorant of the person to whom he or she thinks of committing a MS. it would be wiser to make a few enquiries before doing so.

We demand for literary property the same jealousy and the same resolution to receive just treatment as prevail in all other branches of business.

At present it would seem that too often the author does not, and the publisher cannot, realise that literary property has an existence and a value.

If a man believed his book was an actual property he would not deal with it by methods so vague, unsatisfactory, and unbusinesslike, under agreements teeming with clauses he does not understand.

He would not dispose of his right over it without the

formality of a written agreement. He certainly would not airily hand over to the publisher his rights in other property of a similar kind whose value he does not yet know, and for an indefinite number of years, simply on request.

He would insist upon alleged expenditure being proved to him, before his account was debited with it.

He would insist upon having accounts rendered at the right times, and his executors at his death would similarly insist.

Lastly, if a man thought his MS. was a property in the sense that his watch is a property, what would he do if he found that, in spite of his letters, he could not get it returned to him by the tradesman who had it for inspection?

"What does all this amount to?" it may be asked. "The Society of Authors," the reply might run, "has invited disappointed men of letters to unbosom themselves. This they are notoriously ready to do. As a result, the Society is able to put before the public a few agreements whose provisions are not quite just, and as the Society is not likely to understate its case, it is fair to suppose that these agreements are the most heinous documents in its possession."

It is not fair to suppose anything of the sort. There has been no attempt to "pile on the agony," because it is not in the cause of individual hard cases that we are acting, but against vicious systems which allow such hard cases to be possible.

Many of our members, we are glad to think, are on excellent terms with their publishers, even while they are publishing on systems of which we cannot approve. But it is because the confidence of authors has been so thorough, that now, if certain firms of publishers are asked to verify their figures, they consider the demand an imputation on their honesty.

Neither have the agreements taken as examples been chosen in any way because of their especial reprehensibility.

They were all in their essential principles printed documents,* so that no objection to them on the score of their exceptional character can be made.   Hundreds of luckless authors possess their counterpart.

This has been a protest against systems, and not against individuals.

Surely the protest has been called for.

Surely it is marvellous that such a protest has never been made before.

---

* Save the letters alluded to in Chapter IV., p. 49, and Chapter VI., p. 78 ; but of these letters we have literal counterparts in the office.

FINIS.

APPENDIX.

THE SOCIETY OF AUTHORS.

(INCORPORATED.)

WHEN this Society was first established, the founders were actuated
by two leading principles. First, that literary property requires to be
defined and protected by legislation, and the relations between author
and publisher to be placed upon a basis of equity and justice. Second,
that the question of copyright, especially between this country and
America, is one which requires to be kept steadily in view and per-
sistently attacked.

I. No one has ever denied that the relations of author to publisher
are in the most unsatisfactory condition possible. There are no fixed
principles ; there has never been any attempt to decide on what
principles of equity books should be published ; there are twenty
different methods of publication, not one of which has been ever
advanced on the grounds of justice and fairness to author and publisher alike. Not only are there no fixed principles, but the trade of
publishing is infested and brought into disrepute by persons who live
by preying upon the ignorance and the inexperience of authors,
plundering them in their agreements and cheating them in their
returns.

It is clear that any steps taken with a view to regulate the trade
according to principles of justice and equity should be greatly
applauded by all honourable publishing firms, since they will cause the
weeding-out of houses whose existence is a disgrace to the trade, and

H

will conduce to the improvement of the legitimate book-market by staying the output of a mass of literature consisting for the most part of books which have no *raison d'être*, whose production tends to divert the public from works of a more sterling character.

Such steps as have already been taken have saved a great number of authors from pillage : they have caused thieves, who had grown shameless with their success, to become more careful ; they have awakened a wholesome spirit of distrust in those who send MSS. to publishers ; they have caused a wider recognition of the reality of literary property ; and they have prepared the way for a thorough reform of the whole conduct and management of this branch of literary work.

It is also no small matter that the society has saved many who, having none of the qualities required to insure literary success, would have been dragged in, by lying assurances, to pay large sums of money for what they were informed were the costs of production.

In order to deepen and widen the jealousy with which literary property should be regarded, the Society has in preparation a series of pamphlets which will be issued, as they can be got ready ; three are already in circulation.

Apart from the branch of their work which is concerned with the introduction of equity into the conduct of literary property, the Committee are anxious to do what they can for individual authors under existing conditions. With this view they are ready to advise authors as to the best way to safeguard their property. They examine agreements ; they examine and advise upon accounts rendered ; they have a staff of highly competent readers, who, for a fee, read MSS. and give an opinion upon their literary quality and commercial value ; and in those cases where an author wishes to bring out a work at his own cost, the Committee conduct the business for him, so that he shall not be robbed.

To sum up, the Society maintains :

1. That literary property, already vast, is rapidly growing, and forms a considerable portion of the national wealth.

2. That it is practically undefended, and that it needs to be protected.

3. That the present modes of dealing with this great body of property are based on no principles of right and justice, and leave the door open to every kind of fraud.

4. That it is desirable to awaken a general recognition of literary property, to create a spirit of jealousy over its management, and to introduce the same watchfulness in literary transactions as obtains in all other business affairs.

With this view the Society recommends :

1. That the accounts of publishers should be submitted, like all other accounts between men who have shares in any enterprise, to scrutiny.

2. That authors should be advised as to the best method of publishing, and as to the risks to be encountered.

3. That agreements should be drawn up or examined for authors by an experienced hand.

4. That no author should allow publication to be proceeded with until the agreement is signed.

II. In regard to the question of copyright, it is unnecessary to relate at length the steps which led to the passing of the International Copyright Act of the 25th of June, 1886. This Bill enables this country to enter into any International Copyright Union which may be hereafter established. Inasmuch as the whole question was discussed at length in the last annual report, it seems unnecessary to do more than point out that the Committee are alive to the necessity of procuring the passage of an Act which shall amend and consolidate the existing Acts dealing with domestic copyright (and such a Bill has been drafted under the auspices of a committee of the Society) ; not only because this is urgently required in any case, but to enable this country to enter into an International Copyright Union on equal terms. With reference to that part of the question which is, of course, paramount to English authors—the recognition by America of the claims of English authors to protection in some form or other—it only remains to keep the subject constantly before the Government and the public. We may trust that the authors of America, who are now fully awake to the injury done to themselves by the competition with productions for which American publishers have to pay nothing, will keep the subject alive in the States, and will continue to agitate without any help from us. It is needless to sav that their sympathies are entirely with us, and that they regard tne whulesale and unchecked piracy of English literature as a wrong unworthy of a civilized society, quite apart from the loss which it entails upon themselves. In their case both self-interest and the love of justice compel them to demand the establishment of International Copyright.

The Council call attention to the fact that this *Societv is the only institution which exists in this country for the protection of literature.*

It is, therefore, one which demands the support of every author in the three kingdoms and the colonies. The protection and help it has afforded to authors is every year growing more and more. The Council feel it necessary to state emphatically that substantial progress in their objects will follow in direct proportion, not only as the muster-roll of members includes more and more all living authors but also as the Association comes to be considered the one body which can give advice and assistance to aspirants to the profession of letters. When the Society of Authors can fairly boast that it speaks and acts in the name of the entire body of English men of letters, the mere material interests of the profession will be protected and advanced in a manner hitherto unknown and unattempted.

Owing to the kindness of its legal advisers, the Society is enabled to afford its members skilled assistance and advice which, under ordinary circumstances, they would be quite unable to procure elsewhere without incurring great expense ; and the Society proposes to take up and fight, if necessary, at its own expense, cases which are of a special and typical kind.

The foregoing are the immediate objects of the Society ; other and larger schemes remain for future development.

S. SQUIRE SPRIGGE,
Secretary.

By Order.
January, 1889

CONDITIONS OF MEMBERSHIP.

THE Subscription is One Guinea annually, payable on the 1st of January of each year ; or the sum of Ten Guineas for life membership entitles the subscriber to full membership of the Society.

Cheques and Postal Orders should be crossed 'The Imperial Bank, Limited, Westminster Branch.'

Names of those who wish to be proposed as members may be sent at any time to the Secretary at the Society's Offices. Subscriptions entered after the 1st of October will cover the next year.

The Secretary may be personally consulted between the hours of 1 p.m. and 5 p.m., except on Saturdays. It is preferable that an appointment should be made by letter.

For EU product safety concerns, contact us at Calle de José Abascal, 56–1°, 28003 Madrid, Spain or eugpsr@cambridge.org.

www.ingramcontent.com/pod-product-compliance
Ingram Content Group UK Ltd.
Pitfield, Milton Keynes, MK11 3LW, UK
UKHW012338130625
459647UK00009B/356